# Getting into
# Art & Design Courses

Greg Ioannou and James Foster
13th edition

**trotman | t**

*Getting into Art & Design Courses*

This 13th edition published in 2024 by Trotman, an imprint of Trotman Indigo Publishing Ltd, 21d Charles Street, Bath, BA1 1HX

© Trotman Publishing Ltd 2024

**Authors:** Greg Ioannou and James Foster

12th edn: Greg Ioannou and James Foster
11th edn: Mark Cheeseman and Louise de la Hey
4th–10th edns: James Burnett
3rd edn: James Burnett and Jonathan Hollins
1st–2nd edns: Jonathan Hollins

**British Library Cataloguing in Publication Data**
A catalogue record for this book is available from the British Library

ISBN 978 1 911724 00 1

All rights reserved. This book is sold subject to the condition that it shall not, by way of trade or otherwise, be lent, resold, hired out or otherwise circulated without the publisher's prior written consent in any form of binding or cover other than that in which it is published and without a similar condition including this condition being imposed on the subsequent purchaser. No part of this publication may be reproduced, stored in a retrieval system or transmitted in any form or by any means, electronic and mechanical, photocopying, recording or otherwise without prior permission of Trotman Indigo Publishing.

Every effort has been made to trace copyright holders and to obtain their permission for the use of copyright material. The publisher apologises for any errors or omissions, and would be grateful to be notified of any corrections that should be incorporated in future editions of this book.

Printed and bound by 4Edge Ltd, Hockley, Essex

All details in this book were correct at the time of going to press. To keep up to date with all the latest news and updates and to access the online resources that accompany this book, use this QR code or
**visit trotman.co.uk/pages/getting-into-online-resources**.

# Contents

| | |
|---|---|
| About the authors | vi |
| Acknowledgements | vii |
| **Introduction** | **1** |
| What is this book about? | 2 |
| Routes for art and design students | 2 |
| Who is this book for? | 3 |
| How should I use this book? | 3 |
| **1| Careers in art and design** | **4** |
| Considering your career options | 5 |
| What do art and design graduates do? | 6 |
| Where might your degree lead? | 6 |
| 'Working as an artist …' | 8 |
| 'Working as a designer …' | 10 |
| Further research | 12 |
| Guidance on applying for work experience | 15 |
| **2| Foundation courses** | **16** |
| What can you expect from a Foundation course and why do you need one? | 16 |
| Choosing a Foundation course | 21 |
| Making the final selection | 24 |
| Entry requirements | 26 |
| Checklist | 26 |
| **3| Degree courses** | **27** |
| Where are you now? | 27 |
| What is a degree course? | 27 |
| What can you expect from a degree course? | 29 |
| Entry requirements | 29 |
| Degree course specialisations | 30 |
| Foundation degrees | 32 |
| Degree Apprenticeships | 32 |
| Finding the right course | 33 |
| The final choice | 37 |
| Checklist | 39 |

## 4| Architecture — 40

- Qualifying as an architect — 40
- Entry requirements — 42
- Preparation for your application — 43
- Alternative architecture courses — 43
- The personal statement — 44
- Graduate employment — 50

## 5| How to apply — 51

- Foundation courses — 51
- Degree and HND courses — 52
- The personal statement — 52
- Scottish art schools and colleges — 59
- Non-standard applications — 59
- Preparation for your application — 60

## 6| International students — 61

- Application deadlines — 62
- Portfolio submissions and interviews — 62
- Alternative routes — 63
- English language requirements — 63
- Visas — 64

## 7| Putting together a portfolio — 66

- What is a portfolio? — 66
- Which portfolio should you buy? — 67
- Getting your work together — 67
- Matching your portfolio to the course specification — 70
- Enrolling on short courses — 73
- Portfolio reviews — 74
- Freak-outs — 74
- Foundation course portfolios — 76
- Specialist course portfolios — 78
- Checklist — 82

## 8| The interview — 83

- What is the purpose of the interview? — 83
- What to expect — 84
- Preparing — 84
- The interview itself: some tips — 87
- Checklist — 90

## 9| Offers and what to do on results day — 91

- Foundation courses — 91
- Degree courses — 92
- Results day — 93

| 10| | **Fees and funding** | **95** |
|---|---|---|
| | UK (Home) students | 95 |
| | Living expenses | 96 |
| | Funding your studies | 97 |
| | Postgraduate courses | 99 |
| | The Turing Scheme | 100 |
| | Other sources of funding | 100 |
| 11| | **Postgraduate courses** | **101** |
| | Types of course | 101 |
| | Applying for a postgraduate course | 102 |
| 12| | **Further information** | **105** |
| | Applications | 105 |
| | Funding | 106 |
| | International students | 106 |
| | Art and design bodies | 106 |
| | Architecture | 108 |
| | Reading List | 108 |
| | Magazines | 109 |
| | Websites | 109 |
| | Artists' websites | 110 |
| | **Appendix 1: Institution contact details** | **111** |
| | **Appendix 2: Glossary** | **124** |
| | Studying art and design | 124 |
| | Ways of describing art and design | 125 |

# About the authors

**Greg Ioannou** graduated from the Athens School of Fine Arts in Greece with a First class BA (Hons) in Fine Art, and went on to receive an MA in Painting from the University of the Arts London (UAL). He also studied Set and Stage Design for Theatre Performance at UAL and Technical Theatre at Athens School of Fine Arts. As a qualified teacher, he has been teaching Art & Design, Architectural and Technical Drawing, Byzantine Art (Icons and Fresco) at A level, GCSE, Foundation and university level. He also supervises international and UK students on all aspects of the application process to art college, from preparing for interviews to portfolio construction for Foundation and degree level.

Greg is Head of the Creative Arts Department and the Course Leader for the UAL Foundation Diploma in Art & Design at MPW College. He is also a practising artist and a set and costume designer for theatre.

**James Foster** graduated from the University of the Arts London with a BA in Fine Art in 2016. He has since offered university application and portfolio consultancy to aspiring art students, and has taught art at secondary school level.

James has a continuing art practice in a variety of mediums; currently focused on film, he is exploring, among other aspects, the relationship of film as a physical and non-physical medium to transformative psychological experience and the dimension of the imagination.

# Acknowledgements

This book would not have been possible without the involvement of a great many people. In particular, we would like to thank James Burnett the original author and factual compiler of the information much of which continues to be relevant in this edition. Jonathan Hollins, who was a principal contributor to and driving force behind the first edition of this book, and Beryl Dixon for her work on the second edition and the earlier incarnation of the book. Thank you also to Dariga Alpyssova, Sophia Amaeshi, Nikan Arghandehpour, Annette Bellwood, Jessye Bloomfield, Lottie Chainey, Debbie Cook, Nazar Efendiev, Adam Gold, Robert Green, Honor Hamwee, Sarah Horton, Abdullah Al Kazaz, Annabel Knowles, Saroushka Lok, Birgitta MacDonald, Astrid MacKellar, Lucy May Mahuttanatan, Lucy Mullican, Ella Pound, Holly Ramsay, Anna Roberts, Reinhild Roemer, Haya Abu Al Saad, Andrew Watson and Jess Zhao for their expertise, help, advice and written contributions. Our colleagues in MPW's art department provided contributions to the book and helpful advice on preparing students for their art school applications. Thank you also to Geraint Evans, James Foster, Fergus Hare, Anna Lytridou, Michael Milloy, Alex Mullins and Johanna Parv for their contributions on the rewards and demands of working as artists and designers.

Greg Ioannou and James Foster<br>
January 2024

# Introduction

Art and design is constantly evolving to keep pace with the demands of technology, yet even technology itself relies on the inspirational creativity of artists and designers to fully implement and realise the latest big idea. The most exciting prospect is that you may become a vital contributor to that process. The adventure starts here.

New technologies are creating platforms for humans to communicate and express themselves in new and exciting ways. Artists and designers are necessary in both creating the visual reality of these platforms and in responding to what they mean, how they can be used and how they change us; artists and designers help us to ask what it means to be human in the light of these changes. Artists and designers create social dialogue, explore possibilities and integrate new technological realities into our conception of ourselves. This is just one way in which art and design is at the forefront of changes in our culture.

Ultimately, the latest innovation requires visual guidance, and this has always been a fundamental component since the very first illuminated script and carved hieroglyphic message. In our homes, on our journey to work and in the workplace we are surrounded by ever-changing design and technology. Take a moment to observe some of the objects around you, from the chair that you are seated on or the computer you are using and the desk or table that it rests on – all these have been carefully designed and crafted. We surround ourselves with functionality, and then enhance this environment with our aesthetic choice in pictures and decorative objects.

Art and design graduates go on to have careers in areas as diverse as fashion marketing, art restoration, web design, advertising and architecture; while others take their first steps into producing and selling their work by setting up small design and craft businesses.

In applying to art school you are taking the first step towards what will hopefully become not only your chosen career but also a life journey of experimentation, invention and discovery. Perhaps you already have a strong feeling for a particular discipline, such as fine art, film or fashion and textiles. Or maybe you are unsure which discipline is for you, but just know that your instinct to work with colour, line, form, shape and pattern – to question, experiment and explore – is something that you have to develop. Either way, this book is specifically designed for you.

## What is this book about?

You may be asking yourself the following questions.

- Which course(s) should I take?
- Where should I apply to study?
- What should I include in my portfolio?
- How do I prepare for an interview?

This book offers practical answers to these questions and many others, and aims to guide you successfully through the application process.

## Routes for art and design students

Entry to an art and design degree is usually a little more complicated than entry to other degree courses – that is one of the reasons why this book has been written. Figure 1 below gives an overview of the range of entry routes available; each of these will be examined in detail as the book progresses.

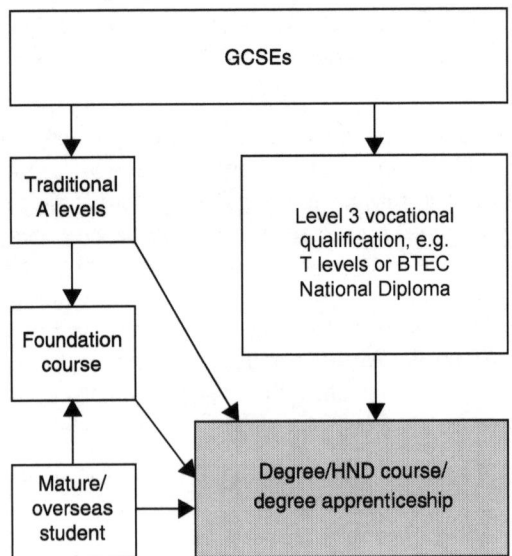

**Figure 1:** Entry routes

## Who is this book for?

This book covers the procedure for applications for both Foundation studies and undergraduate degree courses in art and design, and for students thinking about architecture. If you are currently studying at A level you will find all chapters of this guide relevant. If you are studying for the BTEC National Diploma or a similar qualification, you may be tempted not to read Chapter 2. However, it is recommended that you do read it, because it will help you to know what other students have been up to. The entry routes for architecture courses are outlined in Chapter 4.

If you are a student applying from outside the UK or a mature student, you will have to think about some other considerations. Most of what is contained in this book will apply, and there is additional information in Chapter 6 and the 'Non-standard applications' section in Chapter 5 (see page 59). Throughout the book, the entrance procedures have been illustrated with reference to A levels but the information is equally relevant to students studying for Scottish Highers, the International Baccalaureate or the Irish Leaving Certificate. If you have any questions about whether your academic qualifications will satisfy the art schools, you should contact them directly.

## How should I use this book?

Read it. No, really! Just having the book on the shelf will not get you into art school. Discuss the information and ideas contained within it. Speak to your tutors, friends and parents. You will find it helpful to talk things through. Certain chapters have checklists: use these to help you keep track of your progress. Above all, take action – and when you have finished the book you should have a clear idea of where action is needed. If, for example, you realise that you probably need to do some more life drawing, then go and do some. Admissions tutors are, in any case, always interested in the work applicants have done in their own time, i.e. not just pieces they have done for A level coursework or exams.

You will feel far more confident about your application if you know that you have done everything that you possibly can to help yourself, and reading this book – then acting on what you find out – is the best way to start.

# 1 | Careers in art and design

Wherever you are right now, take a look around you. Look closely at the environment you are in and think about the contribution made to your surroundings by artists and designers. Some may be obvious: there might be a painting on the wall or the light fitting hanging from your ceiling. Look at the clothes you're wearing. Who was responsible for the cut and style? Who designed the fastening on your trousers? Where would you be without that? At home, consider the ergonomic design of your laptop and the artwork for the music that you download on it. Think about the packaging of the food that you eat and the shape of the cutlery that you eat with. Who took the fashion photographs in the magazine that you have just read? Who created the cover design? Who designed the logo? You may have done some research on art schools before reading this chapter – those websites were all designed by someone.

Artists and designers do not just exhibit their work in galleries and exhibitions. They are involved in almost all aspects of our day-to-day living. Artists and designers are concerned with how things look, feel and function. Virtually everything that is manufactured is designed to some extent. Most elements of the media – newspapers, magazines, television, websites, advertising – have considerable input from artists and designers. For every household name that emerges from art school to become rich and famous, there are many thousands of graduates who take up exciting careers that allow them to use their creative talents.

Studying a creative subject will also give you skills and approaches that are valuable in many careers that are not directly 'creative'. You will learn how to communicate using visual information, and you will gain analytical and problem-solving skills. Importantly, by studying alongside other creative people, you will learn to trust your own ideas and to work independently.

If you plan to study something like mathematics at university (but, as you are reading this book, you probably don't!) then you don't need to have a definite idea of what you want to do after graduating, because a mathematics degree can lead to hundreds of different careers other than banking, finance or management, including those that are not directly related to the subject. But a degree in costume for performance, for example, offers you fewer options, so you need to be reasonably sure that a career as a ballet or theatre costume designer is what you are aiming for. Gaining work experience prior to your application is, therefore, not only important in convincing the selectors that you are serious but also will ensure you are heading in a direction that is right for you. If you are passionate about research into make-up, for example, and know that this is the only thing you want to do, then choose the degree course in cosmetic science, rather than something less focused.

Most universities offer excellent careers advice (for example, have a look at the resources section for graduates on the University of the Arts London website: www.arts.ac.uk/student-jobs-and-careers), but in the case of art and design students, it is important to have thought about possible careers before choosing a degree course. This is why the Foundation course is an important aspect of an art education, because it gives you time to look at degree courses in more detail before committing yourself. Many art and design degree courses are very specialised and will give you a relatively narrow range of options, so you need to be sure that you are choosing a degree course that is going to get you where you want to be.

## Considering your career options

A helpful approach when considering career options is to appreciate that the creative skills you possess are key skills. That is to say, your ability to understand and communicate using visual language is as fundamental as being able to understand and use mathematics.

Your talents will always be needed, especially when people are exploring new ideas. Landing on the moon, for example, was a great technological achievement and may not at first seem to have much to do with art and design – but you can be sure that designers were involved every step of the way. Think about it – a footwear designer would have helped to design Neil Armstrong's space boots; perhaps they went on to work for Gucci! Looking at things in this way will help you to keep an open mind.

Most students who apply to art and design courses do so because they have a passion for art, and the ability to be creative. Some students say that their intention, after graduating, is to 'become an artist', by which they mean that they would like to use their creative skills in a way that is not manipulated by financial or corporate issues – perhaps they intend to have their own studio, to exhibit their work and to become respected and admired by those who understand and value what they create. Realistically, however, not everyone has the talent, the focus, the energy or the luck to make a living in this way, but this is only one of the options available to those completing a course in art and design.

## What do art and design graduates do?

A reasonably high proportion of art and design graduates work on a freelance basis or are self-employed (see the section 'Working as an artist ...' on page 8). This can be extremely stimulating and satisfying because you can, to a certain extent, pick and choose the type of work that you wish to undertake. However, it can also be stressful at times because you will need to combine your creative expertise with your skills in business. For some, this is not always a good combination.

Generally, employment rates for art and design graduates are pretty good; most will be able to find work shortly after graduating – although you need to bear in mind that for some this will mean involvement in short-term projects or contracts.

The Higher Education Statistics Agency (HESA) publishes an annual graduate outcomes survey – *What do graduates do?* – which collects data of graduate activity 15 months after their graduation. Data from graduates of the 2020/21 academic year who studied in the Creative Arts and Design field show that, of those who responded to the survey, 49% were in full-time employment, 25% were in part-time employment, 13% were in further study and 6% were unemployed, (www.hesa.ac.uk/data-and-analysis/sb266/figure-10). Further information can be found at www.prospects.ac.uk/careers-advice/what-can-i-do-with-my-degree.

Other art and design graduates were working in a variety of jobs, including marketing, sales, public relations, commercial and public-sector management, buying, retailing, catering and general administrative work. In other words, some were using their degrees as a generalist qualification; others were in temporary employment – just like graduates in other subjects. A list of publications that provide information on careers and employment rates is given in Chapter 12.

## Where might your degree lead?

For the purpose of career options, degree courses can be divided into two categories: the fine arts and the applied arts. Examples of the first category include painting, drawing and sculpture, and some photography and textile courses. The second category includes an enormous range of options, such as communications, fashion design, furniture design, art restoration, jewellery design, television and film design, photojournalism and architectural photography. On many of these applied courses you will be developing skills specifically designed to help you meet employers' needs. If your degree falls into the second category, then you may well find businesses that are looking for someone with your specific qualifications. However, as a fine art student who, say, used digital manipulation techniques extensively in your work, you

1 Careers in art and design

can apply to companies that are as interested in your thorough understanding of that particular software program as they are in your overall digital manipulation skills. This 'cross-over' ability demonstrates the value of key skills and will greatly increase your chances of having a successful working life.

The creative and visual communication skills that art and design graduates possess also make them very suitable for a range of interesting jobs within the field of art and design, such as:

- museum or gallery curator
- museum or gallery guide
- art director for magazines, TV or film
- researcher for TV arts programmes
- arts journalist or reviewer
- arts events organiser.

Figure 2 below will give you some idea of the range of job sectors to which specific degree courses might lead you.

**Figure 2:** Job opportunities

Some of the careers that you might consider are:

- accessory design
- advertising photography
- animation
- architectural and industrial photography
- architectural glass
- art restoration
- art therapy
- book illustration
- branding
- carpet design
- ceramics
- CGI and visual effects
- computer game art

- costume design
- curation
- exhibition design
- fashion design
- fashion photography
- graphic design
- interior design
- jewellery
- journalism
- medical illustration
- model-making
- newspaper and magazine design
- printmaking
- product design
- public arts
- publishing
- sculpture and 3D design
- teaching
- technical illustration
- textile and fabric design
- theatre and performance design
- video and film production
- web design.

## 'Working as an artist ...'

The views of people working as artists included below should give you more of an idea of what to expect and how to make a success of your career. And remember, many artists need to combine their creative work with other jobs, because they cannot support themselves from selling their work. Others choose to combine careers as artists with work in other fields because it helps them to gain a sense of perspective in their creative processes.

> 'There is no one model for an artist's career. Artists face many challenges, but they continue to survive and thrive, and they do this through a range of means. Artists' careers are often cyclical – for most artists, a career has its ups and downs and takes many forms.
>
> 'It all starts in the studio with some fundamental questions that you address through your practical artwork and critical thinking: What kind of work do you make? What are your key subjects/ideas/research? What are your contexts and who are your peers? How do you disseminate your work? Who is your audience? How do you create an effective professional network? Art college can give you the time, space and support to begin to answer these questions.
>
> 'Artists often do a range of things within their practices: making artworks, exhibiting, writing, curation, working in academia, presenting papers, giving talks, etc. Artists can also have opportunities to work with other media outside their core practice or to engage in collaborative or cross-disciplinary projects.
>
> 'Additionally, artists are often also engaged in a range of jobs across the art world and creative industries, both as a way of supporting their practice but also as their predominant career choice: arts administration, artist support, museum and gallery work, art production, writing, teaching, academic research,

curation, etc. It can be very rewarding to have different projects on the go, but establishing a productive balance between your various commitments is a perennial challenge.

'You can't wait for opportunities to fall into your lap, you have to make multiple applications to opportunities posted in listings sites such as Artquest, a-n, Arts Jobs and Arts News, Re-title. You can also initiate your own projects; for example, organising group exhibitions can be a productive first step for early career artists. Many well-known projects and organisations (for example galleries, residencies, studios and workshops) have been initiated by proactive artists to fill gaps and create opportunities and resources where none had existed before.

'It is important to familiarise yourself with the current debates and trends in the artworld by looking at art-related websites, podcasts, magazines and journals, and by attending private views and visiting as many galleries and events as possible.

'Networks of fellow artists and arts professionals are very useful for supporting your career and can be initially established at college with your peers, and then through group shows, studio groups, critical forums, conferences, residencies or through the social side of the art world. Art can be a truly nurturing and fulfilling career that can introduce you to a wide range of engaging people and take you fascinating places. But you do need a degree of resilience, fortitude and resourcefulness.'

Geraint Evans, artist and Pathway Leader for<br>MA Fine Art Painting at Camberwell College of Arts

'I couldn't wait to get to art school and to finally be surrounded by people like me and be given the opportunity to learn about and make art every day.

'However, I think the most important time for me was the year or two straight after I had left. Enjoy art school, and get everything out of it that you can, and as soon as you leave get a space for you to work in and find a way to be in there every day continuing your practice. Make the art that you want to make. Don't concern yourself too much with what other artists are doing. Today we are bombarded with images via our phones, and it's too much, and it's distracting and unnecessary. Don't compare your art and achievements with other people's. You don't have their skills and thoughts, and they don't have yours. Everyone's career is different.

'Let your work evolve. Life changes all the time and there's no reason why you can't be expected to either.'

Fergus Hare, painter

> 'Choosing an art career can be challenging in many ways. However, studying in a Fine Art department will give an emerging artist the confidence that they need to create and believe in their own work. During the years at university it can be overwhelming to have to manage the deadlines of presentations and dissertations alongside making one's work. However, having faith in what you're doing is very important and will help you to carry on your practice after university when the real challenges begin.
>
> 'I strongly advise young artists to find a studio as soon as possible after their studies, and to keep writing, researching and developing their work. Alongside the continuation of your practice, you should also keep applying for opportunities, prizes and residencies. Above all, keep in touch with your peers and fellow artists. Support each other, and organise studio visits and group exhibitions as these social networks will also help to give visibility to your work. Starting a crit group can be a great way to forge new connections.
>
> 'While studying, I'd encourage students to make the most of the resources on offer and be as experimental as possible in trying new techniques and methodologies, as these are difficult and expensive to access once you leave college.'
>
> Anna Lytridou, 3D/installation artist and tutor

## 'Working as a designer ...'

The views of people working as designers provided below should give you more of an idea of what to expect in the world of design, and how to make a success of your career.

> 'At 16, I undertook an Art Foundation in Hereford. This opened up so many possible pathways. I started off in blacksmithing, but went on to jewellery design and manufacture. My further studies at Epsom School of Art and Design intensified my desire to become a jeweller.
>
> 'I was fortunate enough to find employment immediately after completing my studies at Epsom, with renowned silversmith Clive Burr. The work I did for Clive really pushed me as a maker; we worked on projects ranging from high-end fine jewellery for fashion brands to bespoke furniture for interior designers and body armour for films. This early experience played an important part in my jewellery development.
>
> 'After working for Clive for several years, I started my own business. My collections went on to sell in Harrods, Paul Smith and Ally Capellino, as well as in a number of Japanese outlets, including Agete.

'An introduction to the fashion designers Antonio Berardi and Tristan Webber ignited my love of catwalk and statement jewellery, and is where the work I did for Clive years before was so beneficial to me. I applied the techniques that I had learned with him to construct large head structures, exo-back structures and metal stiletto shoes, which were photographed by Helmut Newton.

'This work led me to work with jewellery designer Scott Wilson; together, we were commissioned to create and make collections for Marc Jacobs, Louis Vuitton and Coach.

'Alongside the high fashion work, which has formed the bedrock of my business, I've, more latterly, been able to branch out into the world of film and TV jewellery prop-making, which brings its own creative challenges and rewards and is yet another potential avenue to pursue as a jewellery designer/maker.

'I've always thought that jewellery designers/makers should have to have an open mind – from the way you design, to the way you construct. Keeping abreast of new techniques is also essential to staying ahead of the curve in both your design and within the realms of how production techniques can evolve, always pushing boundaries.

'I've been fortunate that, as well as having a diverse range of clients, I've been able to build up a network of the best crafts people in London, each specialising in their fields. Whether they are casters, setters, engravers, platers, CAD programmers or 3D printers, I know that I can rely on them all to produce excellent work and deliver on time. Establishing a trusted team in this way gives you extra confidence to know that you, in turn, will have a range of processes at your disposal to help you produce work to the highest standard possible for yourself and your clients.'

Michael Milloy, jeweller/maker

Alex Mullins reimagines and handcrafts handsome clothing. Educated at Central Saint Martins and the Royal College of Art, he set up his eponymous brand in 2014. Mullins' clothes take inspiration from real life, editing the everyday to rework the classic wardrobe.

Alex Mullins develops textiles through innovative methods that resonate with the feeling of the 'handmade'. He playfully builds concepts around his clothes, with a heavy focus on cut, colour and distortion.

'If I could give any advice to young people wanting a career in design it would be "NEVER GIVE UP". You will always have drawbacks and disappointments but, as with anything in life, if you want something you have to work for it and don't be disappointed if things don't go your way – just learn from it.

*'Design is a challenging industry, and what I have seen from others in the business in recent times is a brilliant change in attitude. Support each other, be professional and have respect for those around you. When you're good at what you do and have faith in that then there is no need not to work together. Building contacts and connections will give you a well-needed helping hand at many stages of your career, and nurturing these relationships is important.*

*'Most importantly, HAVE FUN, and don't lose your vision.'*

Alex Mullins, fashion designer

## Further research

If you are sure that you want a career in a creative field, but unsure about the exact field at the point when you're trying to choose your degree course, then it might be better to choose something more general, such as fine art or graphic design. In order to get a better idea about possible careers, your research could include:

- doing work experience
- talking to school or college careers departments
- looking at university websites
- talking to practitioners
- visiting professional bodies (such as the Design Council – see Chapter 12 for contact details)
- taking a one-year art Foundation course (see Chapter 2).

### Work experience and internships

If you are considering a career in art or design, you should take every opportunity available to gain work experience, internships or other relevant experience. There are two reasons for this.

1. You will find it easier to convince potential employers and university admissions staff that you are serious about a career or study in your chosen field if you can demonstrate that you have investigated it thoroughly.
2. You will have the chance to see whether the path that you have chosen is right for you.

Getting work experience or internships will require you to do a lot of investigation and to use your contacts, parents' contacts and teachers to help you. Being shy or passive and hoping that opportunities will knock on your door is unlikely to work. Having the courage to demonstrate your talent and creativity to people you do not know is something you will need if you want to have a career as an artist or designer, so as well as being an important part of your journey into art and design, it is also a vital quality for a successful career.

What should you look for?

- Part-time work in galleries, at exhibitions or art shows.
- Part-time work in other creative environments, such as advertising agencies, architecture firms, magazine publishers, fashion companies and interior design businesses.
- Opportunities to help set up school or college art shows.
- Work on blogs, websites or other social media.

*'I started university with a Foundation on the diagnostic course at Central St Martins (CSM), which led on to a specialisation in fashion and textiles with a BA. I am currently a third year at CSM studying textiles design, specialising in print.*

*'I have just completed a year in industry abroad in New York City, where I worked as an intern for Brandon Maxwell, NYES and Teddy Von. I have also worked closely with Richard Quinn on his Spring/Summer 2022, 2023 and 2024 shows, and travelled to India to overlook the embroidery for the shows. Hopefully, I will work with him full-time one day! I am passionate about my chosen subject and am keen to gain experience as well as expand my interests within the field! I take opportunities when and where I can, as I love to network and see creativity throughout London.*

*'I am used to working in a pressurised environment and hold key skills within fashion and textile design. We have learned a variety of different techniques of textiles design which I apply to fashion – pleating and dye are two of my favourites. While I still have so much to learn, I also think that I possess a good eye and have the aesthetic and technical skill sets to bring something new to the table.'*

*Ella Pound, BA Textiles Design, Central St Martins*

*'It is important to expand your experience beyond your art course at school and university and start to think about how you can make a living and career that is both fulfilling and creative, as well as remunerative. For example, while you are a student consider joining a Youth Programme or Youth Advisory Board. Major London galleries such as the Tate, ICA and National Portrait Gallery all have Youth Teams which you may be eligible to join to enable you to actively work in a gallery setting while still a student. Not only will this expand your knowledge of art, you will also gain in-depth knowledge of how a gallery functions, be involved in devising and delivering arts programmes and events, make new friends and connections from an arts environment and also gain an impressive addition for your CV. It will alert you to the wide variety of careers in the Arts sector*

and give you the confidence to network with industry professionals. During your school and university holidays, consider working in a gallery setting or a creative field you find interesting so that you can begin to consider which field of the creative sector you may wish to make a career in.

'Take a look at this website for details on jobs listings, internship opportunities, temporary work and recruitment agencies for students and recent graduates: www.ypia.co.uk/opportunities.

'Many students leave university with little real work experience, wondering how to fill their empty CV. Even a few days' work here and there is better than nothing, as employers will be looking for evidence of commitment, motivation and ambition in the current competitive arts climate. In addition to gaining some work experience, try and get involved in activities at your university itself, such as the students' union, college magazine, socials and Student Ambassador programmes. All of these are great to add to your CV as they show an interest in your subject and evidence of communication skills and willingness to be part of a team. Try and involve yourself in these activities early on, preferably in your first year, before the pressure of exams or degree shows kicks in. Even if you are set on a career as an artist, you may need to support yourself until your own career becomes profitable, so involving yourself in these and seizing the opportunities provided at university is never wasted and may provide another string to your bow.'

Jessye Bloomfield, BA Fine Art, Courtauld Institute

### Advice when choosing internships

- 'Aim for at least three months so that you have enough time to get to know a company.
- Try and find somewhere that pays travel expenses / lunch expenses, as you will not be paid a salary.
- Really research the company you want to intern for and find blogs where previous interns talk about what they did there and what they learnt. I know many people who saved up money to intern in London and then ended up making coffee for three months and learnt nothing.
- Speak with your tutors about the best places to intern as they may have a contact there or have sent students there in the past and can let you know what to expect – my tutor's advice was not to apply to certain companies due to previous bad experiences of past students.
- When interning, if you're not gaining experience in the area you want to be, speak up – for example, if they put you to

*assist the pattern-cutter but you want to be assisting the print designer – which is actually really nerve-racking, but important.*
- *If you work for a small company you will gain experience in all areas and get a much more hands-on approach, but if you work for a larger company you may get to do less but you may have a better chance of getting a job with them after you graduate.*
- *Be as niche as possible – if you want to get into menswear and love digital print, find a company that specialises in digitally printed men's shirts.'*

Annabel Knowles, BA Fashion

## Guidance on applying for work experience

What should you include in your email and covering letter? In the first instance, address your email to someone specific rather than a general title. Attach your covering letter and CV, as emails should be kept concise. For example:

*Dear Ms Smith*

*I am a student studying A levels in Art, French and Geography at St Benedict's School, and am looking for summer holiday work experience in the field of art and design.*

*For further information, please refer to covering letter and CV (attached).*

*I would be most grateful if you could let me know at your earliest convenience if your organisation can offer any work experience.*

*Regards,*

*Jamelia James*

In your covering letter you should include a short profile (approximately six lines) in which you should sound confident and demonstrate your motivation, commitment and enthusiasm. Remember to mention any IT skills, e.g. Photoshop, Lightroom, camera use, etc., relevant to your application. You could also mention an example where you exhibited problem-solving skills – this is applicable to all forms of work experience. State that you are willing to help out whatever the task, and how you enjoy working as part of a team.

Feel free to mention any social media (Instagram, Facebook, etc.) you engage with. Do mention if you have edited or created a web design, a blog, a vlog, etc. Make sure that if you give out your social media links there is nothing on there that would make you regret doing so.

# 2 | Foundation courses

Art and design Foundation courses – the full name is Level 3 Diploma in Foundation Studies (Art and Design) – provide a bridge between the kind of study undertaken at GCSE and A level and the type of work you will do on courses offered at degree level. Although there are exceptions, for those of you currently studying general A levels and hoping to get into art school, taking up a place on a Foundation course will be your next step. Most typically, they are self-contained one-year courses available at a variety of different types of institution, including universities, art schools and colleges of further and higher education.

## What can you expect from a Foundation course and why do you need one?

You can expect to have a lot of fun on the Foundation course. While each course will have its own individual style, all Foundation courses will attempt to challenge and develop your critical awareness and creative skills. A Foundation course will give you an opportunity to discover much more about your creative interests and abilities by giving you the chance to experiment with different fields of the creative arts, as well as explore methods and materials that will not have been previously available to you. You will have the freedom to explore your own ideas and will be truly working for yourself.

There is probably no better way to prepare for a specialist degree course than by completing Foundation studies. The course will develop your abilities and give you more of an understanding of your own direction; it will help you select a specialist area of study, prepare your portfolio and make applications for degree courses. Take a look at the views of these students.

> 'At first, I didn't know what a Foundation course was, I always knew I wanted to study fashion design, but I wasn't sure whether I should opt for textile design or womenswear. Having a year full of experimentation and self-discovery helped me realise my strengths and interests. Coming from Estonia, it was a new experience for me to live in London and it was very intense and exciting. We did a lot of short projects, with deadlines every two weeks. The course taught me self-discipline, and I learnt to organise my thoughts and ideas as

*a designer. One of the most important skills I acquired was keeping a daily notebook and sketchbook, documenting all my thoughts and ideas. My tutors helped me along the way and always knew how to push me in the right direction so that I felt more inspired and creative.*

*'The Foundation year was a good opportunity to meet new people from all over the world. And for many it was the first time away from home. A lot of my current friends and colleagues are people I met on the Foundation course.'*

*Johanna Parv, Central Saint Martins Foundation*

*'I really wanted to study BA Fashion Womenswear at Central Saint Martins (CSM) after studying art, textiles and photography at A level. In order to apply to the BA course, it is compulsory to undertake a Foundation course, which is a great way to get a really good feel for what the BA course might look like. On the Foundation course at CSM, we are being taught how to generate concepts and really look at where our inspiration comes from and how you can harness these inspirations and expand on them. We are looking closely at form of pattern and shapes and different and new ways of structuring, with more than just fashion in mind – it has everything to do with the outside world and what you want your place to be in it. At CSM there's a deliberate absence of rigid rules; instead, a culture is cultivated that encourages thinking beyond conventional boundaries. This foundation programme is instructing us on the art of conceptualisation and probing the origins of our inspiration.*

*'Being at CSM has already brought opportunities to design for real life in hugely exciting ways while being around some very talented individuals who are inspiring and encourage you to constantly bring your best and original work to the table each day. It is giving me an amazing insight into what life at CSM and beyond could look like.'*

*Lottie Chainey, Art (Fashion) Foundation student, Central St Martins*

*'The Central St Martins Foundation Course at UAL stands as an unparalleled opportunity for students navigating their academic journey. When I initially applied, my sights were set on architecture, yet an unforeseen rejection from my preferred university left me re-evaluating my path. Opting for the Foundation course at UAL proved transformative. Rather than narrowing my focus, I embraced a diagnostic approach. Over the first six weeks, I immersed myself in diverse pathways encompassing fine art, fashion, textiles, and architecture. This immersive experience allowed me to make an informed decision about my future career direction. Week by week, engaging with professors across disciplines and scrutinising previous students' works illuminated potential paths. It was during the*

*eighth week that I discovered my passion lay in jewellery, footwear and fashion accessories.*

*'My journey at UAL wasn't just about revelation; it was also about the resources and support that fostered growth. The institution provided an array of facilities – metal, wood and plastic workshops – coupled with experienced technicians who helped translate ideas into tangible creations, mirroring the standards envisioned in my designs. Moreover, comprehensive student support services were instrumental in navigating challenges. Collaborating with the academic support team was pivotal in refining my research skills, understanding the importance of thorough research, and accessing the vast library resources efficiently.'*

Haya Abu Al Saad, graduate, Central St Martins Art Foundation

### How Foundation courses are organised

Colleges vary in the ways in which they organise their courses, but in nearly all cases you will choose from the following areas of study:

- **art:** painting, sculpture and drawing; possibly also film and photography
- **communication:** graphic design, illustration, and film and photography media
- **design:** fashion, product design, ceramics and jewellery.

Course content is standardised to a certain extent, in accordance with the regulations of the four awarding bodies that validate courses in England, Wales and Northern Ireland. These are Pearson, the Welsh Joint Education Committee (WJEC), the University of the Arts London (UAL) and Ascentis*. Under their regulations, Foundation courses are divided into three phases, each phase being roughly equivalent to one of the three terms that make up the academic year. (See Table 1, overleaf.)

The exploratory phase will give you a general introduction to the theory and practice of art and design. You will have the chance to experiment with a wide range of materials you may not have had the opportunity to use before – including plaster, wood, metal and ceramics, for example – and will work on projects designed to help you identify your strengths and interests. In the second or pathway phase you will investigate a specialist area of art and design practice, guided by a tutor experienced in that field. At this stage of the course you will also begin to put together a portfolio for degree course applications.

Last comes the confirmatory phase, during which you will complete your portfolio, work on a major project (usually negotiated with your specialist tutor) and put together an end-of-year show. The build-up to the end-of-year show and the show itself are things that you won't forget. The Foundation course exhibition might, for example, include static exhibits, multimedia displays and a fashion show.

**Table 1:** Summary of Foundation course structure

| Provider | 1st stage | 2nd stage | 3rd stage |
|---|---|---|---|
| Pearson (10 units with some optional units) | Unit 1: Researching, Recording and Responding<br>Unit 2: Media Experimentation | Unit 3: Preparation and Progression<br>Units 4–9 (includes two subject pathway choices in which the following units are completed for each: Information and Interpretation; Personal Experimental Studies; Extended Media Development) | Unit 10: Final Major Project |
| WJEC (6 units) | Unit 1: Drawing and Colour as an Investigative Process<br>Unit 2: Exploring Materials and Making | Unit 3: Developing Specialist Practice and Preparing for Progression<br>Unit 4: Personal Development and Innovation | Unit 5: Proposing and Reviewing a Major Project<br>Unit 6: Curating and Presenting a Major Project |
| UAL (4 units) | Unit 1: Diagnostic Investigation into Creative Practice (Develop knowledge and skills of different art practices) | Units 2 and 3: Developing Specialist Practice (Further exploration, refinement and definition of creative ambitions) | Unit 4: Consolidating Practice (Independent project) |

Sources: www.qualifications.pearson.com, www.wjec.co.uk, www.arts.ac.uk,
*Ascentis only releases the specification to approved centres.

During the final stage you will be expected to produce a personal confirmatory study or project(s).

Although the three stages are followed by all colleges, tutors have some discretion over the way in which students are taught. There are two main methods. During the exploratory phase some colleges allocate periods of time to different art and design disciplines, perhaps one week spent on drawing, followed by another on graphics, fine art, fashion, photography and so on. Others prefer to set projects lasting several weeks, which require students to work in several disciplines at the same time.

Students often fall into the trap of assuming that Foundation courses are totally practical. They are not. At least half a day a week will be spent on contextual studies, including the history of art and design, and you will be expected to produce written assignments, including the creation of a personal statement (sometimes known as a statement of intent) that outlines your final major project.

Another common mistake is to think that studying on a Foundation course will be rather like being at school, with free periods during the day. Foundation course students work hard! Many courses will run from Monday to Friday, often from 9.30am to 4.30pm or later, and may include some evening classes. Your working week will be divided into studio practice, lectures and seminars, visits and personal study time. You should ask on an open day what students' daily schedules are like for the course you are interested in.

Although there are exceptions, Foundation courses often have very large numbers of students, sometimes as many as 400 all following the same programme of study. For people used to small class sizes, this prospect can be daunting. In practice, nearly all students find that they quickly adjust to their new working environment. Many students find that they really feed off the hustle and bustle that comes with working in large groups, and, in part, the course will be about learning to work with others.

Here are some other characteristics of a Foundation course.

- Do not expect lecturers to spend too much time chasing you up. Making the most of the course will be your responsibility. It will be up to you to attend (and a record of attendance will usually be necessary in order to pass the course).
- You will find yourself involved in group projects and can expect to forge strong friendships with your fellow students.
- The course will be exhausting at times but it will also be very exciting.

The view of the student set out below should give you more of an idea of what to expect.

> 'What was different about the Foundation course from studying in school was how much more contemporary the approach to art was. All the students were very energetic and enthusiastic about finding something that was interesting and different. Only at the beginning did we make work according to projects, and very quickly we began to create self-directed projects. Every week we would meet for crits to discuss this work. These were central to the course, and if there was one thing that stood out it was the importance that was given to challenging assumptions of creative decisions; nothing was accepted as self-evident. Discussions were rigorous and the work was often very experimental. This was a challenge because it meant there was not that much support in traditional ways of working. There was not a huge amount of tuition in technique, and the studio was empty when we first arrived; however, it quickly filled with work that was all the more creative and different.
>
> 'Advice I would give would be to be self-directed and to take control in getting as much out of your time on the course as possible (and if you are applying to a Foundation course it is important to show

*that you are this kind of student). You are in a new environment and meeting a lot of new people so it is easy to just accept what is given to you, but part of what you are learning on the Foundation course is to be self-directed; the earlier you can do this the better. Make a point of getting to know all of the facilities that are available to you; there are likely to be some very skilled technicians in different departments that you can learn a lot from, and they will respond well to enthusiasm that you show. Mix with people from other courses, and don't be held back by an apprehension to experiment or try something different.'*

*James Foster, Foundation, Central Saint Martins, Fine Art pathway*

## Choosing a Foundation course

### Getting started

Even though Foundation courses now have a national framework, this may be interpreted very differently by different art schools and colleges, and what suits one student will not be right for another. You can do an initial search on the internet. Have a look at the websites listed in Appendix 1 – the great thing about art schools' and colleges' websites is that they are extremely creative and entertaining. You can spend many happy hours investigating them. They are updated and changed on a regular basis, and, at the time of writing, particularly good examples include the University of the Arts London (www.arts.ac.uk), the Architectural Association School of Architecture (www.aaschool.ac.uk), Kingston School of Art (www.kingston.ac.uk), City and Guilds Art School (www.cityandguildsartschool.ac.uk) and Arts University Bournemouth (aub.ac.uk).

Next, get hold of as many prospectuses as you can and read them carefully. Do not just look at the pictures, but read about the course structure. If you love photography and this does not seem to feature at a college you are considering, you ought to think twice about applying there.

*'I chose Bournemouth for my Foundation because I enjoyed the interview, and because I wanted to be in an art campus as I thought I would prefer being in a creative atmosphere. The tutor was encouraging and I wanted somewhere with a drawing programme as mine was atrocious. I knew I wanted to study fashion for my degree so the Foundation was a bit frustrating at times as we spent a week on graphics, a week on fashion, etc. But in retrospect, the skills I learnt doing this were really useful later on in my degree.'*

*Annabel Knowles, Arts University Bournemouth*

## Course content

Look very carefully at exactly what you will be able to study. Consider the course content: Is it well structured? Is it flexible enough to allow for personal input? What about the range of subjects covered – is there a wide variety? Although Foundation courses are designed to allow you to gain experience across a whole range of disciplines, they do differ from college to college, and so it is important for you to choose a course that suits your needs. If your aim is to study fashion design at degree level, for example, then you will need to spend at least some of your time specialising in this area of study, so make sure that it is properly catered for.

## Location

You can apply anywhere in the country for your Foundation course. However, the majority of students choose somewhere close to home, mostly for practical reasons. These include issues such as accommodation and living expenses, and the reassurance of knowing other people who are at (or have been at) the college. Accommodation, food, travel and materials can be very expensive, and this is a particular issue of concern because a Foundation course is classified as further rather than higher education and you will not be eligible for a student loan. However, UK, Irish and EU students with settled status under 19 years old are not charged tuition fees in further education. (For further information on funding, see Chapter 10.) This is worth remembering, considering the amount you will have to pay for your subsequent course.

It is also worth bearing in mind that Foundation courses are very demanding in terms of time and energy. It is often hard to combine a Foundation course with a part-time job.

There are students who choose to move away from their local area, either because the local college (if there is one) does not suit their preferences or because they want to discover a new environment.

## 'Year Zero'/Integrated Foundation courses

In Scotland, the usual system is for degree courses in art and design to be four years in length, with the first year being a diagnostic course – the equivalent of a Foundation course. Other institutions elsewhere in the UK also offer this pattern; universities that offer this type of four-year undergraduate degree include: Glasgow School of Art, Norwich University of the Arts, Falmouth and Bath Spa. If you like the idea of continuity – not moving to a different university or college after your first year – you might like to look at this option. There are important funding implications, though. Year Zero students are enrolled on higher education programmes – which makes them liable for tuition fees; you will usually pay the same undergraduate tuition fees as for the other three years. You can find further information on funding in Chapter 10.

## Facilities

Questions you may wish to consider include the following.

- How big are the studios?
- Is the light good?
- Will you have your own allocated space, or is it shared?
- What are the IT facilities like?
- Does the college have a well-equipped workshop in which you can experiment with a wide variety of materials?
- Is there a photographic darkroom and studio?
- Will you have access to a ceramics studio?
- Will you have access to specialist studios, or are they exclusive to certain courses?
- What is the library like – is there a wide range of books and a good multimedia section?
- Will you have to pay studio fees, and if so what will they be? (See page 34 for further information on studio fees.)

You should also think about other issues: what are the communal facilities (such as refectories, bars and social areas) like? Some colleges are attached to universities and so you might be able to use their facilities as well. However, this might also mean that the social facilities are not on-site and so some travelling may be necessary.

You will be able to answer some of these questions once you have read the prospectus or looked at the website, but many questions can only be answered by making a visit.

## Open days, visits and speaker evenings

It is vital to attend open days or, if this is not possible because the dates clash with other commitments, to arrange a private visit. The facilities and atmosphere of an art college are the key to whether you will be able to flourish there. Whatever the website says, you will only know whether a particular place is right for you by visiting it. Try to talk to current or ex-students to see what they think of the place. Look at the work that has been produced. Does it excite you? Have a good look at the studios. Check out the facilities – are they really as good as they sound? See if the students are working; a successful studio is one in which people are working effectively – is that the case?

Many schools and sixth-form colleges organise speaker evenings and other special events in which lecturers, course directors and admissions tutors from local art schools, ex-students and other specialists are invited to talk about what to expect when you study art at institutions of further and higher education. Your local college may also offer a talk as part of its open day. Make sure that you go! Information straight from the horse's mouth can be extremely useful: you get the opportunity to evaluate not only what is being said but also who is saying it and how. Most visiting speakers will try to give you a flavour of the kind of work that you can expect to be involved with. Speakers are usually happy to answer your questions, and they may show you slides or a PowerPoint display to give you an overview of what is on offer. These seminars are extremely useful and are not to be missed.

Even though it is always best to attend in person, many universities offer virtual open days/tours. These allow you to ask questions about the course and facilities, and are a good option for international students who would not otherwise be able to see the university in person.

**Atmosphere**

Visiting the college is so important because it is the only way to get a feel for its atmosphere. Most people who enjoy art find that the particular qualities of the physical environment and the ambience of the workspace are vital to their creative processes. This varies from person to person, so you will not find league tables ranking colleges in the order of the inspirational effect that they have on their students. Some people like a buzz around them – lots of noise, activity and excitement; others prefer a quieter, more contemplative environment.

How will you know which colleges are right for you? The only way is by visiting them and talking to students who are studying there. Never choose a college solely because someone else, such as a teacher or a parent, says that it would be right for you. Trust your own instincts about whether or not the atmosphere feels right. You are the one who will have to work there!

## Making the final selection

Using the considerations covered on pages 21–24 will help you narrow your choice down to a handful of institutions. It is sometimes helpful to rank your shortlist in terms of location, facilities, the course, atmosphere, etc. You could give the top college in each category five points, the second four points, and so on. Once you have added up the scores, hopefully some clear winners will emerge. The important thing at this stage is to be honest with yourself about how the colleges match up to your requirements. If a college does not fulfil your needs, then even if going there 'feels' great it will not be. Make sure that you stick to the criteria and try to establish a clear winner based on the facts. You may well find that a couple of colleges are equally suitable and, at that point, gut feeling may help you to make your decision; but as a general guide, stick to facts and not fiction. In other words, do not believe the hype.

## Reputation

Some colleges in the UK are renowned around the world. In some ways, the prestige of these colleges is justified: they attract the most applicants so that they can select the most capable, and this may also be true of the teaching staff as well; they are likely to have good facilities and are located in major cities. As such, you should definitely take a look at them, although gaining entry is very competitive.

However, just because an institution has an excellent reputation does not mean that it is necessarily the best fit for you. It is essential to not base your judgement on reputation alone, but to make sure that you gain a good understanding of what studying at these colleges would be like and whether they suit you by visiting them, and other, less well-known colleges. On your visits, consider the emphasis of teaching, the spaces, and the attitudes of the staff and students to find the institution most appropriate for you.

## Working with your teachers

The final decision on where to go will be yours, but from time to time we can all benefit from a little guidance. Make sure that you work with your teachers. Talk to them. Ask them what they think your options might be. While no teacher is infallible, they will be able to help. Your teachers will probably have first-hand experience of local Foundation courses and will have some information about application deadlines and portfolio requirements. They will know which of the local courses are the most competitive – and whether you would be in with a chance. (Luckily, since there is no limit to the number of Foundation course applications you can make, you can still have a shot at the most difficult to enter while making one or more other applications for safety.)

It is highly likely that your art teacher will be more closely involved with your application than any other person who teaches you, so make sure that you maintain a good relationship with them and try to take full advantage of their expertise.

> **TIP!**
>
> Try to be organised. You will need to create a file or folder to store all the forms and information you will receive. Make sure that you keep your diary or personal organiser up to date. If you do not use one, now is the time to start. The last thing you want to do is miss out on the chance to visit a college because you forgot the date of the open day. Do not try to keep all of this information in your head – you will not be able to remember everything. Before making your choice, make sure that you also read Chapter 7, 'Putting together a portfolio'.

## Entry requirements

As is the case with degree course applications, each institution will have its own entrance requirements for Art Foundation courses. These will be specified in the Foundation sections of the colleges' websites. As well as your portfolio of work, most courses will require:

- 3–5 GCSE (or equivalent) passes at Grade 4/C or above, including Mathematics and English;
- 1 A level (or equivalent) pass, usually with one being an art, design or media subject. Other common qualifications include a BTEC in an art and design subject, or an International Baccalaureate.

Institutions may be able to accept students who do not fulfil such requirements under the proviso that they attend classes in these subjects. If you have any doubts about your eligibility, it is best to contact the college/university directly. Information on how to apply for Foundation courses can be found in Chapter 5.

## Checklist

- Send off for prospectuses.
- Check out websites.
- Confirm dates for open days, visits and speaker evenings – and attend them.
- Draw up shortlists.
- Talk things through.
- Make a decision.
- Make your application.

# 3 | Degree courses

This chapter provides an overview of degree courses in art and design. It aims to give you a feel for what to expect at degree level and discusses aspects of how to find the right course for you. Architecture courses are dealt with in Chapter 4.

## Where are you now?

By the time Foundation students begin the second term of their course, most, though not all, have a fairly good idea of the direction in which their work is heading. Having completed the exploratory phase of the course in which you experimented with a variety of materials and methods across a broad range of disciplines, you will have chosen a specialist area of study such as fashion, textiles, painting, illustration or product design. By this point you will have begun the process of putting together a portfolio and will be considering your options at degree level. Alternatively, you may be a diploma student in your second year of study.

In both cases, you will have begun to specialise in a particular area of art and design practice and will be considering your options at degree level. In some cases, although rarely, you will be in the second year of your A levels and considering making a direct application to degree courses.

## What is a degree course?

An honours degree course is a specialist programme of study offering students the chance to develop practical skills in, and experience and understanding of, a specific area of art and design. Courses offered at degree level will combine practice with theory and, as such, most will require you to undertake some form of contextual studies alongside your practical work. This will vary from institution to institution and may consist of a formally presented illustrated dissertation or some type of multimedia presentation. All courses will show you how to operate within your chosen area of study at a highly sophisticated level. Applications to most degree courses are made through the UCAS system.

Higher National Diploma (HND) courses are generally of two years' duration, and on many HND courses students have the option of transferring to the bachelor's degree (BA) course.

Honours degree courses usually last for three years. Most of them are self-validating. (This means that the institutions offering them have the power to award their own degrees.) In some cases, however, such as in smaller institutions, the degree is awarded by a university which validates the course on behalf of the college. Do not worry if an institution does not award its own degrees. Some highly respected art schools that have international reputations and recruit students from all over the world do not do so. The college's website will give details of the accrediting university.

Although there are exceptions, within the field of art and design there are three broad areas of study available at degree level, and it is from these that you will select a specialist area of study:

- fine art
- visual communications and design
- the applied arts.

Specialisations found within the areas of visual communications and design or the applied arts typically aim to prepare you for the workplace and, in that sense, may be highly vocational in nature. Sometimes they will include a period of work experience. Courses based on fine art, such as painting or sculpture, will be more geared to professional studio practice (although your creative skills may also be valued by industry).

There are essentially four different types of degree you can choose to take: single or joint honours, or a modular or sandwich degree.

## Single honours

Most art and design students studying at degree level in the UK follow a single honours course. Competition for places at well-known universities and colleges is strong. You have to compete to get on a degree course, as there are more applicants than places. In 2022, there were approximately 183,500 applications and only about 36,000 acceptances. UK applicants numbered approximately 148,400, of which about 31,400 (21%) were accepted. International students made some 34,750 applications, of which approximately 4,600 (13%) were accepted.

Courses at colleges with international reputations (and there are many) attract enormous numbers of applications. Places at these institutions are as hard won as for any other type of undergraduate study. Courses typically run for three years and will require you to complete some form of moderated study of the history of art and design. You will have to pass this element of the course in order to be awarded your degree.

### Joint honours and modular degrees

Joint honours courses make it possible to combine the study of distinct but often complementary subjects, such as a BA in Art and Psychology, which is offered by Reading University. Some degrees offer the option to choose from various modules for a portion of the course; these modules may be in a wide range of subjects that are studied alongside art and design. For example, the Fine Art BA course at Central Saint Martins includes a choice of modules as part of the Year 2 Critical Studies programme.

### Sandwich degrees

These may be any of the course types mentioned above, but will also contain some form of structured work experience. Most typically this will take the form of a 'year out' beginning at the end of the second year, in which you will work in industry, returning to complete your studies in the fourth and final year. This will normally be arranged by the university.

*A year abroad*

Some courses provide an opportunity for students to spend a period of time studying overseas. For example, the University of Leeds Fine Art BA course offers the option to extend the course with an extra year studying abroad at a partnered university. For further details, look at the college or university websites.

## What can you expect from a degree course?

Because you will be studying for three years or more and will be concentrating your efforts in a specific area of art and design, on a degree course you can expect to develop high levels of expertise. Degree courses should offer you excellent facilities and technical support within your chosen area and will also provide you with access to resources outside your specialisation, often by means of reciprocal arrangements with other institutions. You will be asked to consider issues and ideas at their most fundamental level and encouraged to fully realise your creative potential. You can expect to enjoy the full range of extracurricular activities that are available to all undergraduates.

## Entry requirements

- The Course Search facility on the UCAS website provides links to all degree courses, and includes information on entry requirements. This will be given in terms of A level grades, International Baccalaureate, Scottish Highers and most recognised international qualifications.

Entry requirements may also be given as a score on the UCAS Tariff – a system of allocating points to academic qualifications. However, for almost all creative courses, a portfolio of work will be the main means of assessment. The university or college will specify that: 'for the first year entry of this course you will be assessed by portfolio/evidence'.

- Information on the UCAS Tariff can be found at www.ucas.com/undergraduate/what-and-where-study/entry-requirements/ucas-tariff-points.

## Degree course specialisations

There is an enormously wide variety of specialist courses available at degree level (see Figure 3). Some disciplines will be familiar to you, others will be entirely new.

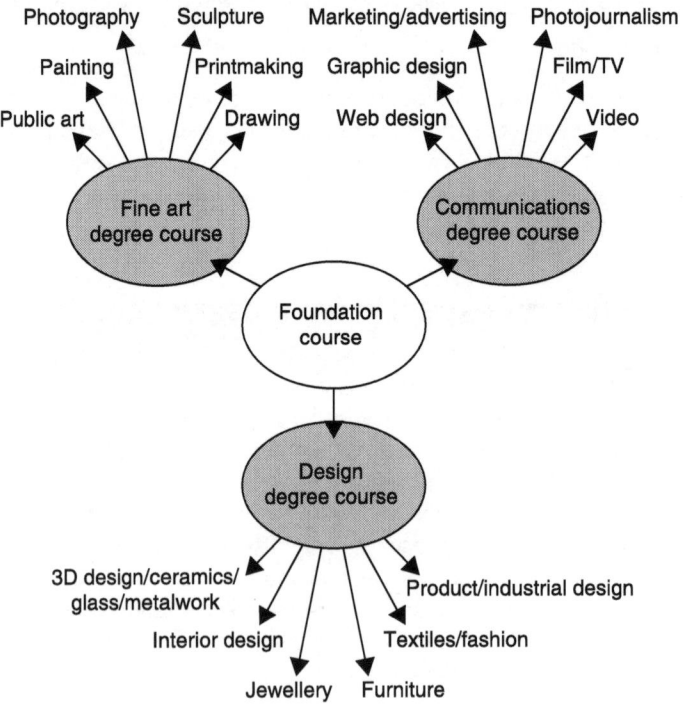

Figure 3: Specialist courses

Taking the three general areas of study already mentioned as a starting point, the following lists are designed to give an overview of some of the courses available. These lists are not definitive – new courses are being set up every year. Please note that some specialist areas of study appear in more than one list. This is because a subject such as photography, for example, could be studied in the context of fine art, with an emphasis placed on personal self-expression, or might be offered as a visual communications course if it concentrates on preparing you for a career in photojournalism.

## Fine art

These courses, which place an emphasis on personal creativity and self-expression, can cover a wide variety of disciplines and often include:

- conceptual art
- drawing
- painting
- photography and film
- printmaking
- sculpture.

## Visual communications

These courses are typically vocational and can sometimes include a period of work experience:

- advertising
- animation
- commercial photography
- fashion marketing
- fashion photography
- film and television
- graphic design
- illustration
- photography
- print and graphic communication
- typographic design
- virtual reality.

## Design and the applied arts

Again, these courses are usually vocational in nature and often aim to prepare students for professional practice:

- architectural glass
- ceramics
- conservation
- fashion
- furniture
- glass
- interior design
- jewellery
- knitwear design
- museum and exhibition design
- performance costume
- product design
- silversmithing
- textiles
- theatre: designing for performance.

## Foundation degrees

So far, we have been talking about honours degrees, but there is another type of degree course available that you might like to consider.

Foundation degrees have been available since 2001 and are on offer in a wide range of subjects. The title is a little unfortunate since they could easily be confused with Foundation courses! The new courses are a qualification in their own right and can also lead on to an honours degree course. Designed in consultation with employers, they are courses that train people in specialist career areas and develop:

- work skills relevant to a particular careers area
- key skills, for example communication and problem-solving
- general skills, such as reasoning and professionalism.

If you do a Foundation degree you will be able to choose between entering employment and continuing training in your job, or converting the qualification into an honours degree through further study, usually by transfer into the second or third year of a related degree course. Foundation degrees are available in a range of disciplines, including graphics, fashion, product and furniture design, game art and design, CGI and visual effects, hair and make-up, and interior and architectural design. A full list of courses and more information can be found in the Foundation degree section on the UCAS website (www.ucas.com).

## Degree Apprenticeships

The vocational higher education market is growing in the UK, with more emphasis placed on teaching practical skills alongside qualifications, with a view to addressing the high-level skills gap that exists in certain industries. This allows for the combination of full-time paid employment with part-time study, enabling students to have the benefit of experiencing both work and study. Art and design technology are commonly fields that lend themselves well to Degree Apprenticeships. There are currently over 60 universities implementing Degree Apprenticeships in the UK and the number of employers signing up to the scheme is growing.

### Some examples of Degree Apprenticeships

- Architecture
- Automotive design
- Ceramics
- Costume and wardrobe
- Fashion and textiles
- Jewellery

- Photography
- Product design.

How much will a Degree Apprenticeship cost? Nothing. Employers are expected to cover the cost of apprenticeship training. This will, however, mean more competition for places. NB: You are not guaranteed a job at the end of a Degree Apprenticeship, but you will be guaranteed to be employable within a skills-based sector, which will give you a significant advantage. Consult www.prospects.ac.uk/jobs-and-work-experience/apprenticeships/degree-apprenticeships and www.ucas.com/apprenticeships/degree-apprenticeships for more information.

## Finding the right course

Most students applying for places on specialist degree courses either are attending or have been to art school. Perhaps you have been studying close to home and want to move further afield, or perhaps you are well established where you are. You may have a pretty good idea of what you are looking for, but try to keep an open mind. Do your homework. Get hold of as many prospectuses as you can and read them carefully. Don't just look at the pictures; read about the course structure and content. If you plan to study furniture design, for example, and love to make things in the workshop, make sure that the courses you are considering are supportive of this approach. Use the internet – the great thing about art schools' and colleges' websites is that they are extremely creative and entertaining. Information on how to apply for undergraduate courses can be found in Chapter 5.

### Course content

How will you know which course is going to suit you? For example, what is the difference between studying a BA in Glass and a BA in Architectural Glass? Degree courses in specific subjects will differ from college to college. Some illustration courses, for instance, will place more emphasis on digital manipulation while others will focus more on traditional drawing techniques – so it is important for you to understand exactly what is being offered.

Take full advantage of the literature available. Make sure that you read and fully comprehend the course specification. If you are unclear about anything, try to speak to the course director or head of school. Look very carefully at exactly what will be studied, at what point in the course and for how long, and how much flexibility and choice you will have. For example, if you want to become a forensic photographer, make sure that you are not applying to a fine art photography course!

Since many art and design graduates work freelance, it is important for them to understand how to run their own business – about finding premises to work in, tax and legal requirements, and how to calculate costs when pricing their work – and how to market their work and present it to prospective employers or buyers. If you think you may freelance in the future, ask now whether the course contains modules on self-employment, given either by course tutors or by the college or university careers service.

> 'I can still remember the day I got my offer from Chelsea College of Art for the BA in Textiles design. All the effort I had put into my studies at MPW had paid off.
>
> 'I had always been told that university involved a great deal of independent practice and the ability to complete multiple projects at once is the most important and basic skill. In the beginning, I was worried about the sudden change of unsupervised learning and how that might be difficult, but my experience at Chelsea was that, although the work is self-motivated, this gave me the chance to discover my passions and push myself out of my comfort zone.
>
> 'Every tutor and technician were very responsible and engaged; they have rich experience and knowledge in their field and always provide guidance according to the preferences of each student.
>
> 'Over the three years, I learnt lots of new skills: the use of domestic and industrial knitting machines, stitch techniques, embroidery, weaving, printing; and we always had the opportunity to get knowledge from the other subjects to enrich our own practice.
>
> 'Thinking and solving problems was a huge learning curve, but having peers to discuss ideas with was priceless.'
>
> Jess Zhao, BA Textiles with Knit, Chelsea College of Art

## Location

You can apply anywhere in the country, or even abroad, for your degree course. Consider the practicalities of your course location, such as the cost of accommodation and travel. Moving to a big city may be attractive, but will you be able to afford it? Many students enjoy and benefit from the dynamism that city life can offer; some prefer to live and work in a quieter location. What will be right for you? For many students it is essential that they are close to galleries and museums. What are the local facilities like? Do they meet your needs? Higher education is expensive and, although you may get some financial help, nearly all students have to raise funds privately. If you are planning to work part-time, are there job opportunities?

'My time at New York University was truly transformative. The dynamic atmosphere and innovative approach to arts education in the NYU Studio Art programme provided me with a unique and enriching experience. The talented faculty and diverse student community fostered a creative environment that encouraged exploration and pushed boundaries. The influence of New York City goes far beyond the classroom, and has left an enduring imprint on not just my artistic prowess but it has also significantly shaped my perspective on the world.'

Adam Gold, BA, New York University

## Facilities

Does the college have the facilities that you will need to study your subject? A degree-course studio should be very well equipped. Make sure that the relevant technology is up to date and kept that way. As well as working within your own field you may well need to cross over into other areas of art and design. Many art schools have reciprocal arrangements with other institutions. Do these exist and will they be practical? If, for example, you intend to study sculpture, you will no doubt be looking for spacious, well-lit and well-equipped studios, but what about the IT facilities? Remember that you will have to put together some kind of contextual study. Are the computers up to the job and could you use them to create 'virtual' sculpture?

As your skills develop, so will your needs. Try asking yourself the question: 'Do I know what all the equipment is for?' If you do, then the course is probably not well equipped.

You should also think about communal facilities such as refectories, bars and social areas. Some colleges are attached to universities, and so you might be able to use their facilities as well. However, this might also mean that the social facilities are not on-site and so some travelling may be necessary.

## Student support

Does the institution provide good welfare arrangements, such as student counsellors and an accommodation office?

## Additional costs

Your tuition fees are unlikely to cover all of the costs of materials that will be needed for the course; these include art materials, printing and other costs essential to the course. The course website will often give details about the extra costs you can expect to spend; most universities describe these as being around £200–£500 per year, and may be higher in the final year.

Some institutions may charge students studio fees, which are fees paid to the university for some of the costs of materials and facilities, these can vary considerably from place to place, but are not likely to be more than £200 or so each academic year. If the course you are considering does have these fees, it is worth finding out what the fees are and what facilities you get for the money (this is not always set out in prospectuses or course leaflets). You could also check – perhaps by asking a student on an open day – whether the final degree show involves students in much expenditure. You will be able to answer some of these questions once you have read the prospectus or looked at the website, but many questions can be answered only by making a visit.

## Open days and visits

It is only by visiting a department that you will get a feel for its atmosphere. Most artists and designers find that the physical environment and the ambience of the workspace are vital to their creative processes. This varies from person to person, so you will not find league tables ranking colleges in the order of the inspirational effect they have on their students. But ask yourself: 'What is the vibe like?' It might suit other people, but will it suit you? Make a point of talking to students who are studying there. Is the working environment a productive one? Can you picture yourself in it? Never choose a college solely because someone else says that it would be right for you. Trust your own instincts about whether or not the atmosphere feels right. After all, you are the one who is going to study there!

If you are an international student visiting the UK, it may be worth arranging a private tour, as many institutions can arrange this. Otherwise, book a place on one of the published open days or virtual open days.

## Past students

It is always interesting to look at the names of practising artists who have graduated from the university or art school. Although famous alumni do not necessarily make one institution better than another, they can act as a guide to the type of work that is being undertaken there. And if an artist you really admire studied on one of the courses you are investigating, this can add to the attraction of the college.

## The final choice

Remember that you are going to have to live with this decision for three or four years, so try not to be carried away by a sudden rush of blood to the head. As important as it is to trust your instincts, using the steps outlined above to narrow down your choice to a handful of institutions will help you make a decision you won't regret.

Go through this list and think things over carefully. Talk things through with the people who know you best – you will benefit from a second opinion. Rank your shortlist in terms of location, facilities, the course, atmosphere, etc. Try giving the top course in each category five points, the second four points, and so on. Use the scores to help identify which course meets your requirements. You will probably find that there are two or three courses that are up there. Don't be afraid to trust your instincts, but make sure that your shortlist is based in reality and not fantasy. Read the views below on making that final choice.

> *'I am currently studying the BA Jewellery Design course at the University of Arts London – Central Saint Martins. My journey into this field began during my A levels, fuelled by a deep fascination with gems and stones. Beyond their inherent preciousness and beauty, I am fond of their intricate structures and how they seamlessly integrate into jewellery pieces. Transitioning from my initial fascination with aesthetics, I have come to understand that jewellery design is beyond mere ornamentation; it encapsulates profound concepts and pursues a commitment to environmental sustainability. My A level aspirations to secure a spot in the BA Jewellery Design course were not just about education; they were the foundation for my ambition to establish my own brand and business. Designing jewellery has proven to me it transcends a creative endeavour; it requires responsibility, discipline, commitment and the ability to be innovative, qualities that drove my pursuit of realising my ambitions.'*
>
> *Saroushka Lok, BA Jewellery Design, Central St Martins*

> *'Studying at Central Saint Martins was like riding a creative rollercoaster. On my BA Textiles Design course, I dove into print, where every project was a new chance to play with patterns and colors. The place buzzed with energy, and it was all about trying out wild ideas and seeing what stuck. Now, on my MA Material Futures course, things are getting even cooler. It's like exploring uncharted territory, mixing up tech and eco-friendly vibes. The whole experience is more like hanging out in an artist's dream lab than sitting in a classroom.*

*I am making some great mates, laughing a lot, and picking up a whole new perspective on design. It isn't just about getting a degree; it is about growing into a more creative, chilled-out version of myself. I can't wait to see where this journey takes me next.'*

May Mahuttanatan, MA Material Futures Art, Central St Martins

'As a current Year 1 student at London College of Communication (LCC) on the BA Animation course, I am satisfied with the experience so far. University offers a range of useful facilities, from access to libraries or studios with computers and drawing tablets, to various software, including Toon Boom and Autodesk Maya, which are industry-standard in animation production. Tutors and lecturers have experience in industry, and can often answer questions related to finding work placements. We get a lot of help, especially from our head of department.

'However, it is a place for those who are ready to learn independently. Briefs, explanations and instructions are always given at the beginning of every project. While students are welcome to ask any question regarding upcoming projects, the university expects almost full independence from students, the ability to use given materials and learn on their own. This helps to develop creative thinking, but may not suit for some students.

'Overall, I made a great choice to study in LCC, and am looking forward to many exciting animation projects in the future.'

Dariga Alpyssova, BA Animation, London College of Communication

'After graduating from MPW, I received offers from all my UCAS choices. I chose to study Interior Architecture and Design at London Metropolitan University because it has a good range of real-life projects and is forward thinking.

'The London Met offers me exactly the things I learned to value at college: communication, encouragement of individual creativity and respectful interaction. The teachers are friendly and always willing to help, which contributes to a positive and calm learning environment.

'At the same time, a high standard is demanded without creating competition between students. Given the impact on university education by the Covid-19 pandemic, this is an aspect not to be underestimated, as tutors are sometimes the only people involved with the course we can see. I appreciate not being one of many and having a personal relationship with my lecturers.

'The projects we have worked on so far always have a personal component and combine historical backgrounds with new design. Above all, I enjoy my studies because I learn theoretical and technical things as well as practical ones.

'The things I learned in MPW I now use as a foundation in university. Art and design can be everywhere and in everything, you just have to train your eye to see it.'

Reinhild Roemer, BA Interior Architecture and Design,<br>London Metropolitan University

'I'm currently studying in my first year of a BA in fashion design at the University of Edinburgh. So far, I have already learnt so much about pattern cutting and constructing garments. The course is very creative and allows you to go in your own direction, but also focuses largely on skills and pattern cutting; this is great, as being able to create patterns and make garments is a very useful skill to have in the fashion industry. I highly recommend this course to anyone wanting to study fashion design as it teaches you a wide range of skills that will prepare you well for life after university.'

Honor Hamwee, BA Fashion Design, University of Edinburgh

## Checklist

- Send off for prospectuses.
- Check out prospectuses, university guides, etc.
- Check out websites.
- Confirm dates for open days, visits and speaker evenings – and attend them.
- Talk to tutors.
- Draw up shortlists.
- Talk things through.
- Make a decision.
- Make your application.

# 4 | Architecture

There are a number of possible routes for students who wish to apply for architecture courses. Applications for some courses, such as those offered by art colleges, are made in the same way as for other art and design courses; but you can also apply to study architecture at university without the need to do a Foundation course, or at private institutions. These routes are described in this chapter.

Of all the different manifestations of art and design that we encounter in our daily lives, the work of architects is, along with that of clothes and product designers, the one that people come into contact with most often. Every shop, office building, fast-food outlet, cinema, bridge or multi-storey car park that you see on your way to school or work has been designed by an architect. The work of some architects is immediately recognisable: London's 'Gherkin' and The Shard, Paris's Pompidou Centre, or Bilbao's Guggenheim museum spring to mind. But your home was also designed by an architect, as was your train or bus station.

To practise as an architect in the UK you need to gain registration with the Architects Registration Board (ARB). This takes a minimum of seven years after you leave school. But don't be put off by this if you are interested in architecture because this does not mean that you will spend seven years in lectures; although you will have to attend some lectures, the seven years involve a combination of academic study and work experience in an architectural practice. If you are interested in architecture and want a shorter course so that you can work within the fields of architecture or related subjects such as interior design, then there are other, shorter options available. This chapter will explain the different routes available to you.

## Qualifying as an architect

### Registration with the ARB

In order to gain registration with the ARB, you need to pass three stages, which are overseen by the Royal Institute of British Architects (RIBA – incidentally, if you are serious about becoming an architect, try to visit the RIBA's London headquarters, which holds many exhibitions as well as being home to an impressive architecture bookshop). A typical route to gaining registration is shown in Table 2 (opposite).

**Table 2:** Typical registration route

| Year | Programme | Stage in the RIBA process |
|---|---|---|
| 1 2 3 | Bachelor's degree in architecture – BA, BArch, BSc or equivalent (see below) | Part 1 |
| 4 | Work experience | |
| 5 6 | Postgraduate study – Dip Arch, MArch or equivalent | Part 2 |
| 7 | Hold RIBA Part 1 and Part 2 and have at least two years' work experience (12 months of this experience should be in a UK/EU practice). Professional Practice examination | Part 3 |

## Choosing a course

If you are going to embark on the journey towards becoming an architect, you need to think carefully about the first three years of the course. There are a number of options and the right one for you will depend very much on your academic and creative strengths. There are about 60 universities in the UK that offer three- or four-year undergraduate degrees in architecture (usually UCAS code K100 or K101) that will give you exemption from RIBA Part 1. There is a section on the RIBA website that lists these institutions (see Chapter 12). Some of these are more geared towards students who are interested in the structural as well as the creative aspects of architecture, and these often require A levels in Mathematics and/or Physics.

Other universities concentrate more on the creative aspects of architecture and so require A level in Art. In some cases, history of art can be an advantage if the course has a significant focus on the historical side of architecture. You will often hear people talking about 'the language of architecture'; in the same way that there are rules – which of course can be broken – governing the construction of sentences when we speak English, architects use architectural elements in the design of buildings. Some of these are new, but often they are based on historical ideas. Just as we mix old and new words in a sentence, architects can mix old and new architectural details in a building. For entry onto these courses, you will be judged on your portfolio as well as on your academic achievements or predictions. In addition to the above entry requirements, some universities also set a practical task.

If you are reading this before choosing your A level (or equivalent) subjects, then spend some time looking at the entrance requirements of university architecture courses to ensure that you will have the right subjects to apply for the type of course that will suit you best. If you are already studying A levels, then you still need to do this research to ensure that you do not waste choices on your UCAS application. The UCAS website 'Course Search' facility is a good starting place, as the list of K100/K101 architecture courses has links through to the universities' entrance requirements. If you are already studying A levels and you are not doing the right subjects for an application to study architecture, you have two options.

- Take an extra year on your A levels, and add the necessary subjects. Some further education colleges and a number of independent sixth-form colleges will offer a fast-track one year A level programme.
- Think about following an Access course or an art Foundation course. The universities will be able to advise you on what alternatives to A levels they might be prepared to accept.

## Entry requirements

When looking at entry requirements for architecture courses, you should be aware that while these will specify particular grades or scores at A level, International Baccalaureate, Scottish Highers or international qualifications, the universities will also be looking at the following.

- Is the candidate genuinely interested in, and suitable for, architecture?
- Is the candidate doing the right subjects?

Some universities will also set an additional entrance test or creative task in order to assess the applicant's creativity.

> **WARNING!**
>
> Do not assume that if a university requires, for example, AAA at A level and you are confident of achieving these grades, this guarantees a place. You would first have to get an offer of a place (either conditional upon achieving the grades, or an unconditional offer if you have already achieved the grades).

### Diploma courses

An alternative to the university route described above is offered by the Architectural Association (AA) School of Architecture in London. The AA is, as its name suggests, a specialist architecture school and it offers a Foundation course for students with a limited art background, a three-year course leading to RIBA Part 1, and diploma and master's courses for students wishing to qualify as architects or to pursue postgraduate studies in architecture.

For entry to the Foundation course students can apply with one A level at A*–C. If you apply with only one A level, it must be in a non-art/design subject. So, you cannot apply with an A* in Art and Design or Product Design or similar. You must also provide your GCSE certificates or the equivalent for study in Year 10/11 (this is usually grade 9–10 if you are an overseas student). Please note, EU and international students without settled or pre-settled status will have to apply for a visa after they have been offered their place on the course. More information can be found on page 64.

## Preparation for your application

Architecture courses are oversubscribed. For 2022 entry, according to UCAS, there were around 5,900 places available for architecture and over 35,300 applicants; so it is important to be able to demonstrate to the admissions staff that you are a serious applicant.

For international students, the figures are even less encouraging. For 2022 entry, around 1,070 international students (of about 10,000 applicants) gained places.

In order to make your application as strong as possible, other things you should do prior to the application include:

- reading books on the history of architecture, and on contemporary architecture
- doing some research on the uses of, and properties of, common building materials such as glass, steel, concrete, stone, etc.
- background reading on a favourite building or structure (preferably one you have visited)
- visits to exhibitions
- keeping a small notebook with you, in which you can make notes and sketches of buildings that interest you.

And, of course, all these things will be mentioned in your UCAS personal statement. See below and Chapter 5 for more details.

## Alternative architecture courses

Not everyone who has an interest in studying architecture wants to practise as an architect. There is a whole range of other careers that involve architecture, including:

- administration work in an architectural practice
- local council planning
- architectural model-making or computer-aided design
- architectural photographer

- interior design
- structural engineering
- teaching.

There are several courses other than the K100 degrees mentioned in the previous section that can lead to careers associated with architecture. For example:

- courses at art schools, such as the three-year BA in Interior Architecture and Design at Arts University Bournemouth or the BA in Interior and Spatial Design at Camberwell College of Arts
- engineering-related courses, such as structural or architectural engineering
- art history courses.

Entry on to some courses may require the student to have completed an art Foundation course (see Chapter 2).

## The personal statement

A personal statement for entry on to an architecture course should incorporate the following sections.

- Why are you applying for architecture?
- What have you done to investigate architecture?
- How are your A levels (or equivalent) or other courses relevant?

Remember, the personal statement is limited to 4,000 characters.

### Personal statement 1 - Architecture degree application

I developed a passion for structures and spaces in my early childhood. My favourite hobby was assembling Lego® blocks. As my eyes examined the sketches and instructions, my mind imagined the pieces forming together to create a high-rise building, a fancy race car or a bold 12-wheel truck. Whether they be shiny or dull, square or round, big or small, these blocks lined up to form my next masterpiece!

As I grew older, I discovered that it is not only the assembly of structures that fascinates me, but the design and creativity behind them. I decided early on that I wanted to design such structures for people to occupy, enjoy and admire. I have come to gain interest in what makes a structure unique to the observer, not simply to my own eyes, but to the eyes of others who view the physical attributes of a building differently. Seeing the 'finished product' and the sense of contribution would become my reward.

Today, I draw anything that challenges my imagination; from cars, to buildings, to nature. Colours excite me as they challenge me to investigate the right combinations to achieve the best results. I continuously experiment with tools and techniques, such as markers for rendering, pencils for sketching, and airbrushes for specifics. Through this, I have found that patience is a key to artistic expression, as it underscores the importance of planning, reviewing and contemplating.

I have been exposed to diverse cultures and civilisations, and found myself drawn to how diversity has influenced architecture and landscape throughout history. It is my opinion that architecture reflects the historic evolution of civilisation, the development of man, and man's interaction with the environment. I view architecture not only in terms of the physical structure or the 'art in buildings', but as individual objects that mirror the architect's personality, his or her dreams and aspirations.

During the summer break, I had the opportunity to gain some work experience in London with Map Projects. This has allowed me to closely observe an architectural firm in operation. I attended two site meetings, witnessed negotiations, and participated in discussions with architects that opened my eyes to new perspectives and creative ideas in design concepts with a focus on continuously exceeding clients' desires. I also worked with Dewan Architects in Dubai; observing design production from concept through development, sustainability, and use of materials. I have also interfaced with fresh graduate architects, enriching my view into the world that I aim to make as my career.

The blend of mathematics, physics and art and design within my A level studies has provided me with the critical elements to pave the path for my university study. Mathematics has reinforced the importance of essential numerical and problem-solving skills. Physics has taught me the essential conceptual limitations of architecture in relation to the laws of nature and matter. Art on the other hand, has allowed me to express myself freely, and go wild with my ideas without any limitation.

I worked on several models, from concept to execution and finishing. I have experimented with materials such as clay, wire mesh and copper wire. Exploring with these materials translated my undefined ideas to innovative 3D models, while maintaining precision, context and simplicity.

During the past few months, I have visited multiple universities where I explored their respective programmes and interacted with professors and students to enlighten my choices on the courses that will help me to be my very best. I am fully committed to studying architecture. I am innovative, hardworking and accountable. Studying architecture will be the best fit for my interests and capabilities and will allow me to explore the endless possibilities to influence the well-being of humankind while also challenging the established norms.

### Personal statement 2 - Architecture degree application

I first realised I wanted to study architecture at a young age, as I was always constructing toy buildings and sculptures. I especially enjoyed toys that gave me the freedom to create whatever I wanted.

I was touring with my choir in Barcelona when I visited Parc Guell. I loved the fact that each shape was based on nature and so different to other local parks or housing. I went on to study Gaudi's work as I was interested in how the walls and pillars he designed were influenced by nature.

Studying Gaudi's works led me to the world of Art Nouveau, which captivated me. Paul Hankar is one of my favourite Art Nouveau practitioners because his work is extremely detailed both in terms of architecture and the artwork built into his designs. One particular factor that makes Art Nouveau interesting for me is the handrails, particularly those that embed naturally inspired art into their design. The flower shop is my favourite of Hankar's designs because of the way he uses natural, flowing shapes.

My interest in Art Nouveau led me to explore architectural forms which it has influenced, such as Art Deco. I fell in love with the symmetry and perspective of the buildings which were brought from the 'expeditions to the ancient world'. The juxtaposition between the modern and ancient was fascinating because they were using certain ancient motifs in their art to make something unique.

Growing up in the dense, urban area that is Tehran, I was surrounded by soulless buildings, where cost-effectiveness and 'Westernisation' were the major considerations, with Iranian culture completely discarded. This sparked my interest in the duality of the interior and exterior of buildings; after reading Thiis-Evansen, my understanding of experienced qualities of architecture increased. I appreciate the works of such writers who use a phenomenological approach to emphasise the lived experience of architectural structures rather than focusing solely on their material properties. However, there were notable exceptions in Tehran, where the buildings incorporated the elaborate arabesque motifs of Safavid architecture alongside modern Brutalism. An example is the Azadi Tower, built to recognise historical identity and values by the orders of the Shah.

Yazd is a perfect example of an ancient city that was engineered to work in the extreme heat. Yazd lay on the Silk Road and was a resting place for the caravans. The buildings have an ingenious cooling system of *badgirs*, or wind chimneys, that take hot air in and make it into cool air that can be dispersed into living spaces. Modern cities, which will be affected by climate change, could benefit from these ancient systems, which are effective and environmentally friendly.

Whiteread's exhibition on negative space made me think beyond what I can see and touch. Her exhibition made me think about three-dimensional space differently. I realised I could achieve a similar two-dimensional effect using a film camera. I especially liked her work on the negative space of buildings, because by taking a modern house and filling it with concrete she made the interior look Brutalist. It's interesting to see something that has a given personality change as its negative space is shown. In a way, the negative space changes the architectural style of the building.

I worked for a structural engineering company once a week for a year. I also taught in a workshop on how to make tensegrity models, which made me a better leader and teacher and I got to learn more deeply about the nature of different tensegrity models.

I've been on my school's student council for two years, being the information officer and vice president. I helped with charities and I ran a debating club for the GCSE students in our school.

### Personal statement 3 - Architecture degree application

My passion for architecture rooted from the creative freedom and the joy brought to clients as a result of one's work. Though it had progressively, through time, been driven by the importance and significance architecture plays on our environment and the power it has on elevating and enhancing cities and countries. Architectural response to climate change and its continual threat to our environment is what has intrigued me most, and I have been inspired by architects such as Laurie Baker. He resorted to indigenous, traditional ways of design, through the use of local resources, to consequently reduce his structures' carbon footprint. Buildings like the Centre For Development Studies are testimony to Baker's law that 'architecture should merge with the surrounding landscape, rather than be standing out. It should not compete with nature but be in harmony with it.

As someone of Ethiopian heritage, I have been exposed to Baker's style of architecture and the wider integration of vernacular and biophilic architecture, as its presence has been preserved through history and continues to contribute to the cultural architectural style of today; from the Sidama to the Dorze huts, both of which utilise the surplus materials in surrounding environments. Through visits to the Dorze region, I witnessed the use of grass, a renewable insulation material, which was stuffed between interwoven bamboo that was covered by banana leaves, acting as roof shingles. I found the locals had attempted to minimise the use of linear structures and used beehive and elephant heads as primary structural inspiration, expanding further on their link to nature and its attempted preservation. This triggered my realisation that the most inexpensive of buildings that we design seem to be most practical and suitable to the surrounding environment; applying Baker's principle that 'cost effective hours are not always for the poor'.

Through further study in art, I have become more aware of the threat that the rise in sea levels poses to the future of human existence. I am fascinated by architect Koen Olthuis's response to such threat: the mass construction of floating houses and their ability to move to accommodate space and adjust to the changes in water level. Having been inspired by Olthuis, I used my physics knowledge to experiment with structural adjustments. I began to look at a buoyancy system, a structure's ability to withstand imbalances in weight, an anchor system and attempts to become energy self-sufficient; I concluded with the study of tensegrity platforms. Tensegrity platforms are an elegantly sophisticated piece of physics that give an alternative solution to the use of air tanks. Unlike air/water tanks, these platforms do not require calibration and adjustments; they maintain equilibrium regardless of the distribution of weight. The careful consideration of weight and its distribution ignited my research into the use of cedar wood in beams and cladding; its lightweight and environmentally friendly nature provides a better alternative in energy sufficiency and makes it a dimensionally stable, highly weather resistant wood.

I believe the endless design possibility rooting from Olthuis's initial concept has created hope for both the future of architectural development and the future of human life on earth. Such structural understanding and interest in materials, had stemmed from my work experience at AM Meri architecture firm. I am excited to utilise my passion and determination to better serve the architectural field, while learning from the best to expand my existing knowledge and understanding.

You will have noticed that the applicants have dropped a number of hints as to what they would like to discuss at the interview, by mentioning ideas, buildings and architects. If they are lucky, the interviewer will be interested in hearing them expand on these topics, and so they will be able to talk about things they have already prepared. For example, they have mentioned:

- colour
- architecture and civilisation
- 3D modelling
- use of materials
- work experience.

In order to impress the interviewer, they would need to do a good deal of research into the things they have touched on in the statement. If there is one thing guaranteed to create a bad impression at the interview, it is being unable to talk about things in the personal statement.

> 'I'm an architecture student at Central Saint Martins. In my experience, working in an arts-focused university has helped me push myself to compete creatively with other students. I've made friends from other courses who give me different perspectives on both my current projects and their designs and proposals. The environment at the university helps us to create a wider conversation with each other about the problems popping up globally, be they political or environmental. I would say the greatest experience I've had at this university has been the allowance of failure, because it has enabled me to adjust my angles of approach to the problem at hand and helped me grow. This road is hard however, and it means you will have to have the drive to push forward and succeed, no matter the disappointments that may set you back.'
>
> Nikan Arghandehpour, BA Architecture, Central Saint Martins

'My journey to architecture simply started with drawing in my free time. During A level Art, my interest and passion towards architecture drastically increased. With the help of my tutors, I was able to produce artworks of an exceptional standard that led to an astonishing portfolio and offers from most of my university choices. I chose the AA because of its richness in experimentation, concept and processes. The first year taught us the fundamentals of architecture: how to draw plans, sections, create 3D models, and produce architectural diagrams to convey our research and ideas such that the quantity of information delivered is not overwhelming to the viewer. As our tutors always used to tell us: "Quality over quantity", and "Make sure a 10-year-old can understand what you are trying to convey. Only then will your project be successful." I joined an experimental unit in my second year, where the brief was to design a mixed-use high-rise tower with a set of *programs of my choosing. I chose a labyrinth of casinos. I particularly enjoyed that year and it opened my eyes when I realised almost any crazy/fictional idea can be developed architecturally. I am now in the third year, where the experimental brief is to design a museum or a series of them along the OXCAM arc, working through site-selection, context and providing for what's needed – another level of excitement and joy unravelled. History and technical studies sweeten the course even more. Architecture is an incredible field. Let your imagination pave your path.'*

Abdullah Al Kazaz, BA Architecture,
Architectural Association School of Architecture

'The AA has two identifiable and unique strengths: An embrace of the use of a vast assortment of method and media within projects and an all-encompassing holistic approach to architectural education. It exemplifies the term "association". A community in which students, tutors, lecturers, workshop assistants and librarians can come together, cooperating in the synthesis of ideas.

'You might not know everyone, yet the sense of belonging to a single, unified body of creative minds is ever-present.'

Nazar Efendiev, BA Architecture,
Architectural Association School of Architecture

**WARNING!**

Do not copy any of the personal statements in this book: they are only intended to be a guide. You might be tempted to get external help in writing the personal statement. While you should get advice from as many people as you can, you should not get someone else to write it for you or use Artificial Intelligence (AI) software. There are websites that offer (for a fee) to prepare the personal statement for you, but be aware that UCAS uses sophisticated anti-plagiarism software to check each statement, and if it detects that the work is not your own, your application may be cancelled.

## Graduate employment

The Higher Education Statistics Agency (HESA) collects data on what graduates do after they have completed their studies. Data collected for the 2020/21 academic year shows that for students who studied architecture, building and planning, 89% of those who responded to the survey were in some form of employment and 13% were involved in some form of further study, including those working and studying.

Source: www.hesa.ac.uk.

# 5 | How to apply

This chapter explains the procedures for applying for Foundation, degree and Higher National Diploma (HND) courses. However, before you apply, you need to do lots of preparation. If you have not already done so, you should read the relevant sections on choosing a course in Chapters 2, 3 and 4.

## Foundation courses

In most cases you apply directly to the art colleges for entry to their Foundation courses, and you can apply to a number of colleges simultaneously, since there is no central application scheme.

The application forms vary from college to college. All require basic details about yourself and your education, but they differ in the amount of space (if any) that you have to write about yourself and your interests – i.e. the personal statement (see page 52 for details).

Unlike the UCAS scheme for applications to degree courses (see page 52), there is not one date by which all applications must be submitted. The closing date for applications varies from college to college, and so you must do your research early and make sure that you do not miss any deadlines. The closing date for applications is often the end of January, but this is not true for all colleges, so consult the prospectus or the website well in advance.

Most Foundation course applications need to be accompanied by a reference, usually from the head teacher or head of art at your school or college. If you are a mature student or are not studying art at school, you should read the section for non-standard applicants (see page 59). Warn the person you choose to do the reference well in advance that you are going to apply, and ask them whether they are willing to act as a referee. References usually take time to write, so do not surprise your referee with a form the day before the deadline. Even if he or she does manage to write it in time, it is less likely to be full of the necessary detail, and it will certainly not emphasise your planning and organisational skills!

Bear in mind that you are applying for a place on a practical course, so the application form is only the starting point. The key elements of the selection process are the portfolio and/or the interview. Admissions staff will place most emphasis on evidence of high potential and creative ability. See Chapters 7 and 8 for more information. If your initial application is successful, you will be asked to deliver (or send) your portfolio to the college so that it can be assessed by the selectors, or to attend an interview at the same time as your portfolio is reviewed or later.

## Degree and HND courses

If you are applying for honours degree courses, Foundation degree courses or HND courses, you normally do so using the UCAS system.

Almost all applications are made online using the UCAS Hub. Further details can be found on the UCAS website and in the book *How to Complete Your UCAS Application* (see Chapter 12), but a brief overview of the process is given here.

The deadline for UCAS undergraduate applications is 31 January at 6pm (courses at Oxford and Cambridge have an earlier deadline of 16 October at 6pm). In total, you can choose five university courses.

Further details are available on the UCAS website, or from the institutions themselves.

## The personal statement

Applications through UCAS will require a personal statement. You need to plan this very carefully, as it will significantly affect your chances of gaining an interview or being offered a place.

The UCAS personal statement is currently undergoing reform, and changes are due to be implemented in 2026. It appears that these changes will include the personal statement being broken up into more specific sections, the aim of this appears to be to make the writing of the statement, and knowing what information is important, more straightforward and less ambiguous for students. Reviewing these changes now may be useful for gaining further clarification on what is best to include in your statement. Further information can be found at: www.ucas.com/about-us/news-and-insights/reforming-admissions.

Many application forms give you enough space to write 300–500 words in support of your application, and the UCAS online application form gives you 4,000 characters. They generally specify the information that they are looking for. For example, the application webpage for the Central Saint Martins Foundation course suggests you describe why you have selected the course, your future plans, your current work and the work you would like to make on the course.

As you have a limited word count, your statement needs to be planned carefully. A good response might include a list of your particular interests, but you must make sure that they are relevant to the course you are applying for – there is no point in writing too much about your love of textiles if you are applying for a Foundation course that specialises in photography and media.

You should try to cover the following.

- Introduction: reasons for wanting to study art.
- Reasons for choice of college.
- Interests within art: areas of art that you enjoy, e.g. fine art, graphics.
- Influences: artists who inspire you, exhibitions that you have seen.
- Description of some of your own recent work.
- Career plans or future areas of specialisation, if known.
- Other information: interests, work experience, travel.

> **TIP!**
>
> Attending open days or degree shows is important if you are to convince the admissions tutors that you are serious about your application. More information about open days is given on pages 23 and 36.

The best way to demonstrate your enthusiasm for art is to talk about your own work. This also gives the admissions staff an idea of your interests in a specific, rather than general, way. It is a good idea to try to include a contemporary artist, as you want to show the selectors that your interest in art is a developing one and that you are keen to be part of the current art scene rather than immersing yourself wholly in the past.

> **Personal statement 1 – Foundation course**
>
> Your course appeals to me as an opportunity to explore my personal practice by learning new skills and working with other students. I frequently incorporate concepts from science and art into my art projects, and was awarded the Science and Art Sixth Form Scholarship.
>
> I am fascinated by microbiology; in my current art project I am experimenting with photos I took through a microscope lens. One

photograph was highly commended in the Royal Academy Youth Summer Exhibition and is displayed on their website. My work with cells translated itself seamlessly into the medium of etching, inspired by Norman Ackroyd's misty, ethereal prints, which became central to my A level work. I entered my AS final piece into the UpStArt competition; it reached the final round, was displayed at the Strand Gallery and auctioned for charity.

I am also intrigued by textiles and, by working as an apprentice this year for a Japanese designer, alongside my A levels, I have realised the importance of responding to a medium by working with its personality; use a fabric's grain line, explore its strength and accept its unpredictability. Furthermore, your Foundation course would give me the option of experimenting with new ideas or specialising within the area of fashion and textile design, and most importantly, access to resources and advice from tutors and exposure to other students' ideas.

### Personal statement 2 – Foundation course

Within Frida Kahlo's painting *What Water Gave Me*, Kahlo demonstrates a release of self-expression, as she illustrates a reflection of her life through the medium of art. When considering this painting, Kahlo encourages you to think about the context, giving you a greater understanding of her as a person, while allowing you to make personal connections with her artwork. I would like to consider what would be placed within my bathtub.

Gently floating in my bathtub would be a houseboat on which I used to live. On the houseboat would be my Dutch father, Mancunian mother, four sisters and me, each of us expressed within our own passions: literature, drama, politics, sport, dance and art. Throughout my life I have always been surrounded by culture, visiting many art galleries and the theatre often. However, over the years I have learnt not just to appreciate art through culture, but I have been encouraged to understand the skills that go in to making it. Studying History of Art has given me a deeper understanding and a historical context, increasing my understanding of art in terms of technique, meaning and reason, as well as defining my style. This understanding allows me to heighten my appreciation of the subject.

The houseboat would be moving across to a vibrant and decorated location – Spain. Spanish culture has featured strongly in my life. Here, I am dancing flamenco with my four sisters. Flamenco dancing is something I have trained in for ten years; and is on a parallel with how I view my art – I see flamenco as another form of release, encouraging and illustrating my personality.

Near to my feet on the opposite side of the bathtub would be the Tate Modern, which I have visited throughout my childhood, and is where my initial passion for artists such as Madame Yevonde, Matisse, Frida Kahlo and my continuing passion for art as a medium have flourished. I was selected by Tate Modern to join their Raw Canvas team where, following training, I have become a staff member and now play an active role in the development of the Youth Programme. This involves organising events to get young people involved with art; while also undertaking research trips to places such as Paris and New York to look at how they run their youth programmes. Being a part of the Raw Canvas team has provided me with skills such as outreach, event organisation, education, interpretation, marketing, access, how to talk about art, and the study of both the role of the curator and the role of the artist; encouraging me to find ways to get other people involved, by seeking out different dimensions and perspectives that people can relate to.

Sitting on the rim of the bathtub is me holding a camera. For work experience I have been working as a production assistant for Gilly Booth at Hijack Films, on a documentary they are making about Eduardo Paolozzi. Part of my role was taking production stills; this was a great opportunity as I was able to take photos of the interviews as well as Paolozzi's artwork firsthand, which were being kept in private collections. This experience provided me with an insight as to how the medium of film and film industry is run. I am really happy to be doing A level Photography, as the medium was featuring a lot in my artwork and now I have the chance to execute it in greater depth.

I would love to be a part of the Foundation Diploma in Art and Design that you offer at Manchester; as within my art work I have always been keen to experiment with a broad range of techniques, exploring different mediums in greater depth, in order to broaden and enrich my style, and to gain a greater understanding of art as a subject. Also studying in Manchester has a pull on me, as it is where some of my roots lie.

## Personal statement 3 - Foundation course application

My love for fashion and art was initially born out of admiration for the people who use their creative platform to drive a form of activism; the way they take something as simple as the fibres we put on our bodies everyday and don't use it to conform or integrate themselves in social acceptability but use it as a form of creative anarchy. This came from something as small as Gaultier putting men in skirts to Renate Bertlmann transforming the idea of garments and accessories into an avant-garde feminist statement. From here I developed a huge aesthetic admiration for the way in which this was represented by people like Hussein Chalayan who takes unambiguous objects and redefines them to represent something new in a rebuff to the world around him, such as his AW00 collection; 'Before Minus No'. To me this took fashion from simply being the cloth that meets the eye to becoming one of the most prominent forms of social commentary.

As I began to learn and experiment within textiles and fashion I developed a passion that I could invest into my work, not only allowing it to be beautiful but for it to represent something meaningful. My approach to textiles is quite tactile, I find compelling to take embroidery and simple fabric manipulation techniques, such as trapunto, cross shirring and smocking, and utilise them in a manner that creates an abstract outcome. My ability to compile these unusual elements and manipulate them to create a piece that represents more than meets the eye is fascinating, surprising others and sometimes myself as it often leads me to a place I did not expect it to go.

I have chosen to study an art Foundation course in textiles and fashion as I still feel I have a lot to learn; there are many areas of textiles and fashion I look forward to experimenting with, such as knitwear, further embroidery and garment design. I am really interested in beginning to learn the art of translating an idea or concept and materialising it into a 3D garment that complements and expresses the silhouette it's placed on with the use of the techniques I will be learning. I have found that designers such as Rei Kawakubo and Yohji Yamamoto have inspired my interest in employing the human form and engineering my work in a way that doesn't necessarily complement it in the classic sense but instead reconstructs it. Through this, dispelling the idea of normal that has been engrained through societal pressures.

I have been lucky enough to have the opportunity to do an internship with the creative production agency Sylvia Farago Ltd, where I dealt with the production of editorials and campaigns for clients such as Top Shop, Adidas, Stussy and Vogue. The creative inspiration I have got from being surrounded by some of the most important people in fashion has helped to refine and mature my aesthetic and understanding of fashion itself. Through moving my knowledge away from only the technical side of textiles and fashion, I have learnt how the industry itself works and my eyes have been opened to the different opportunities available. Due to this I have been lucky enough to understand quite early on that my path lies in fashion design and styling. The fundamental understanding of the way in which the garments fit, the effect of different fabrics and manipulation techniques that I will gain from an art Foundation will help me to discern what these aspects of a garment can evoke, thus helping me in my pursuit of both design and styling.

Notice that the personal statements include details of artists that the applicants are interested in. Never drop in the names of artists or galleries/exhibitions that you have visited without giving some indication of why they are important to you. The point of the personal statement is to demonstrate that you not only enjoy art in a practical sense, but also think about it.

### WARNING!

Do not put things into the personal statement simply to impress the selectors. If you do get to the interview stage, you may be asked to talk about one or more of the artists or exhibitions that you have mentioned, and the surest way to be rejected is to be caught out. You might be tempted to get external help in writing the personal statement, and of course it is a good idea to get advice and feedback from teachers, your parents and anyone else who can help. You may be aware of the many websites that offer to prepare the personal statement for you, for a fee. UCAS uses anti-plagiarism software to check each statement, and you may have your application cancelled if it appears that the work is not your own.

Similarly, it may be tempting to use Artificial Intelligence (AI) software to write your personal statement for you, but UCAS will be able to use software that can detect if a passage is written by AI. Furthermore, while these methods may help to create a statement that looks well written, it will not have the same meaningful content about you, and university admissions teams will not be impressed by a well written statement that says nothing specific.

Another key element in the personal statement should be something to lead the reader to ask you a specific question at interview for which you have prepared an outstanding answer. In the UCAS application examples above, the applicants describe, briefly, their own work, but cannot give much detail. They can be reasonably confident that, if invited to interview, they will be asked more about these pieces of work, and so they can prepare for this part of the interview in advance.

### Individuality

The sample personal statements shown above are well structured and demonstrate the applicants' interest in art and what they have done to find out more. But remember that if you are applying to art schools, you are intent on following a course that requires creativity and an ability to convey what is inside your head into things that other people will relate to or want to use. So do not be afraid to be, as someone involved in admissions at one art school puts it, 'quirky' in what you put in your personal statement. If you have interesting ideas or interesting ways of demonstrating your passion for art or design, by all means use them. This could take the form of an anecdote, a quotation, an event or piece of art that inspired you, a poem, a dialogue ... anything that helps you to show your creative side and where your ideas come from.

### What to avoid

The personal statement is just that – a statement that reflects your interests and influences. There are some things to avoid at all costs.

- You must avoid using very general statements that say nothing about you. 'I have always been interested in art, and get great enjoyment from my work', without an explanation or description of specific areas of interest or pieces of work, will not give the selectors anything to go on.
- Writing 'I would like to come to your college because of the facilities' is too general: say which facilities and why they attract you. Bring in your own areas of interest if possible.
- Never make judgements about artists, their work or exhibitions without backing them up: 'I went to see the John Craxton exhibition at the Dorset County Museum and I liked it' is not going to impress anyone. The admissions tutors would be more won over, however, if you added 'because it was fascinating to see how his paintings and prints were influenced by lesser-known artists who lived there. Craxton had cousins who lived locally and so he was exposed to a variety of painters whose work was based around representing the landscapes around them. This inspired me to look at other British artists who also worked in the South West, including John Piper.'

## Scottish art schools and colleges

As already mentioned in Chapter 2, the system in Scotland is slightly different: most degree courses are four years in length and incorporate the equivalent of a Foundation course. In some cases, students can enter the second year directly if they have undertaken a suitable Foundation or portfolio preparation course. For details, you should contact the institutions directly. In both cases, application is made through UCAS.

## Non-standard applications

Not everyone who applies for Foundation courses is an A level (or equivalent) student. Similarly, some people apply for degree courses without having studied on a Foundation course. The main categories of 'non-standard' applicants are mature students (for further and higher education purposes, anyone over the age of 21) and overseas students. If you fall into one of these categories, you should make direct contact with the colleges that interest you to discuss your situation. Many applicants who are not classed as 'mature' or 'international' students but who nevertheless do not have the 'standard' qualifications for entry gain places on art courses every year. It may be because they took A levels in, for example, science subjects; or they left school at 16 and went to work. If you are in this situation, the first port of call will be the art schools, which will be able to give you advice about their particular requirements. This might involve some short courses, evening classes, a 'pre-Foundation' course (see page 63) or other relevant preparation.

The colleges' websites and prospectuses will also contain sections aimed at you. It is important to be aware that, for all applicants, in addition to your personal qualities, the portfolio is the most important element in the application. Without a promising portfolio, you will not be offered a place. Make sure that you read Chapter 7, which offers detailed advice on this.

### Mature students

You may already have either a portfolio of work that you undertook when you were at school (in which case, it will probably need updating), or perhaps a collection of pieces that you have been working on recently. It is often helpful to get guidance from art teachers, and for this reason many mature students will take evening classes, portfolio classes or Access courses before applying. (Sometimes this is best done at the college to which you intend to apply.)

Application to postgraduate courses is covered in Chapter 11.

## Preparation for your application

Make sure you stand out from the others.

- Visit galleries and exhibitions on a regular basis.
- Keep a notebook and a camera/smartphone with you at all times to record things that interest you.
- Try to get your work exhibited in school exhibitions, your local library, local cafes – anywhere where people will see your work.
- Try to arrange some relevant work experience – this could be in a gallery, a museum, an art studio, or with a designer or an architect. Getting work experience in a creative field is not always easy, and you will need to use your contacts to find out what opportunities might be available and how best to approach them – use your friends, friends of friends, your friends' parents, your parents, your parents' friends, your teachers, your teachers' friends – anyone who can help!

'By being given the opportunity to study textiles at A level, I was able to have the chance of starting to explore the world of fashion from a textiles point of view. Fortunately, we were taught at a very mature level which has made it easier for me to transition from A levels straight to a BA in fashion design. By developing a close relationship with my tutors, I was not only able to enjoy myself but also produce outcomes that challenged my skills. By being set work for specific deadlines, it has helped me with the university workload and my time management. Through the help of my tutors, I was lucky enough to have the opportunity to intern for Julien MacDonald for his SS19 collection, which was an amazing experience.

'I am in a much larger creative environment now, where I am surrounded by so many talented individuals. I am so fortunate to have the opportunity to study here. Although the workload is considerably larger than A levels, I know that everything I am doing now is a step closer to my career in the industry. Studying fashion design at university is tough, there is a huge amount of not just work but also the immense amount of research that goes into being able to produce final outcomes that are backed up by evidence and interest.'

Holly Ramsay, BA Fashion Design, Ravensbourne Art College

# 6 | International students

Students from all over the world come to the UK to study on art or design courses. Many UK institutions are recognised internationally as being the best in the world. In 2022, over 4,500 overseas students gained places on art or design degree courses. Many of these students will have followed Foundation courses in the UK for a year. If you want to be a fashion designer, an architect or a product designer, or if you want to train to work in the creative sides of TV, film, IT or advertising, studying in the UK will give you the best possible preparation and qualifications.

Following Britain's withdrawal from the EU, European students (EU, EEA and Swiss) are now considered international students. They are no longer granted Home fee status or eligible to receive loans from Student Finance, and will have to be granted a visa to study in the UK. Unless exempt (see below), European nationals will have to apply as international students.

Exemptions only apply to those with Irish citizenship or European nationals who have successfully applied to the EU settlement scheme. There are also some special categories applicable to circumstances, such as humanitarian protection and victims of abuse, that allow for Home status equivalent eligibility.

In response to these changes, many institutions have introduced more scholarships and other financial schemes available to European students, so it is worth enquiring about your eligibility for these. The institution to which you are applying will normally be able to offer support and advice for European students regarding these rules.

The majority of unsuccessful international applicants fail not because they are not committed to or not suitable for their course, but simply because they are not fully aware of how to submit a successful application. Since you are reading this chapter, you have already increased your chances of success significantly!

NB: Students who are interested in architecture may already be aware that the regulations for architectural training in the UK mean that UK architecture qualifications will allow them to work anywhere in the world. A significant proportion of the most exciting and high-profile architectural projects around the world in recent years have had an input from architects trained in the UK.

Most of the information contained in this book applies to international students as well as to Home students. However, some aspects of the application procedures are different, and if you are applying to study art or design at Foundation, degree or postgraduate level you should be aware of this. The main differences are listed below:

- application deadlines
- portfolio submission and interview process
- alternative routes
- fees (details can be found in Chapter 10)
- English language requirements.

## Application deadlines

You should read the information on application routes and deadlines contained elsewhere in this book. Information on the application deadlines will be given on the individual institutions' websites. In some cases, international students can apply for these courses later than Home students, and the dates for interviews may also be later in the year.

## Portfolio submissions and interviews

In order for you to be offered a place to study art or design at an art college or a university, someone from that institution will need to look at examples of your work.

Most institutions will ask that you submit an online portfolio, and you may be interviewed via an online video call, but some institutions will have in-person portfolio reviews and interviews. Some institutions may also have representatives in other countries that you can apply to instead of applying directly; this will allow you to have an in-person interview.

The University of the Arts London offers several online and in-person short courses, specific to a variety of subjects, that are tailored to portfolio preparation. These typically cost around £500. This is a good way to experience learning at an institution as well as increasing your chances of a successful application, so it is worth checking whether an institution you are interested in offers such a course.

Under some circumstances (e.g. if you are considered to be too young for direct entry onto a Foundation course, or if your English is not sufficiently good) you may be advised to spend a year on a pre-Foundation course at a recommended school or college in the UK before proceeding to the Foundation course (see opposite).

## Alternative routes

Most international students follow the same route as UK students to their degree or postgraduate art and design courses; that is, a one-year Foundation course followed by a three-year BA course and then, in some cases, an MA course. Some universities, such as Norwich University of the Arts (www.nua.ac.uk), run four-year degree programmes to ensure that international students are fully prepared. UAL offers a six-month, online, pre-degree course for international students. Completing this course will guarantee a place on undergraduate courses specialising in art, design and communication (excluding fashion, textiles and jewellery).

Pre-university art education varies considerably in content and delivery from country to country (for instance, in the balance between technical skills and original ideas), so some international students are not accepted directly onto Foundation courses. Others may have the potential to start a Foundation course but they may be too young or may not reach the required standard of English. Students in this situation may be advised by universities or art schools to spend an extra year in the UK prior to the Foundation course.

A popular route is to spend a year in a UK school or college either following an art pre-Foundation course (an art and design-related course together with, if necessary, English classes) or studying on one-year accelerated A level courses. This route would be recommended by the university or art school at the interview or portfolio review stage. Many art schools will have partner institutions that can provide these courses.

An alternative route for those international students who are too young to go directly onto an art Foundation course is to attend the International School of Creative Arts (ISCA), an independent boarding school near London, which opened in July 2009 in association with the University of the Arts London. The school provides pre-university training for British and overseas students to prepare them to enter a university course in the arts and related disciplines. In addition to two-year A level courses in a range of art and design subjects (with the option of adding academic subjects in combination with these), the school also offers a one-year portfolio programme, designed for those who possess the academic qualifications for university entrance but need to develop a portfolio. It also offers an online Foundation diploma. Further information can be found on the school's website (www.isca.uk.com).

## English language requirements

You should refer to the individual institutions for their requirements. To give you an idea of what level of English is required, the University of the Arts London asks:

- Foundation diploma, pre-degree online: IELTS 5.0
- Bachelor of Arts undergraduate: IELTS 6.0
- Master of Arts: IELTS 6.5
- Master of Research: IELTS 7.0

Information on IELTS (International English Language Testing System), TOEFL test and other accepted English language qualifications can be found on the UK Council for International Student Affairs (UKCISA) website – details in Chapter 12.

## Visas

For many international students, a visa is necessary to be able to study in the UK. The type of visa and the English language requirements necessary to obtain the visa vary from course to course, and are liable to change periodically. The university and college websites will give details of what they ask for in terms of English, and will also give guidance about visa issues.

Students from outside the UK will usually need a student visa (also referred to as the 'student route' of application) to study in the UK. You can apply online for a student visa on the gov.uk website or at a local visa application centre, which are listed on the gov.uk website.

Nationals from the EU, EEA and Switzerland are considered 'low risk applicants', and as such do not have to submit as much information as applicants from other regions when applying for a student visa. (Irish nationals and European nationals with settled status do not need a visa to study.)

To apply for a student visa, you:

- must have an unconditional offer of a place on a course. Once you have been offered a place, your institution will send you a Confirmation of Acceptance for Studies (CAS) reference number. You must have a CAS reference number before making a visa application. If you have more than one offer, you must decide where you intend to study and use the CAS from that institution when you apply
- may need to prove your knowledge of the English language (reading, writing, speaking and understanding); there are some exemptions to this, including if you are from or have previously studied in certain countries considered as majority English-speaking countries or have studied at a school in the UK
- may need to show evidence of possessing sufficient finances to pay for one academic year's fees. You may also need to show you can afford living expenses when staying in the UK:

- £1,334 per month (for up to nine months) for courses in London
- £1,023 per month (for up to nine months) for courses outside London.

A student visa application costs £490. You will also need to pay the immigration health surcharge of £470 for each year of the visa for which you are applying. The institution at which you are intending to study will be able to offer guidance on the visa application process. Further guidance can be found at the UK Council for International Student Affairs (UKCISA).

# 7 | Putting together a portfolio

For most students making the move into further or higher education, the offer of a place is normally made on the basis of past academic performance, personal statements and references, predicted grades for forthcoming examinations and, increasingly, an interview. With art school applicants, all of the above applies but with one very important addition: you will need to show your work in a portfolio. Above all, colleges want to know who you are, what you have done and, most importantly, what your potential is. Demonstrating these things is the function of the portfolio.

If you are interviewed alongside your portfolio submission (discussed in Chapter 8), you will deliver your portfolio, the college will look at it and in the interview you will get the chance to talk about it and yourself, as well as to ask and answer questions.

For some this may seem a daunting prospect. Most artists worry about showing their work to others. It is not surprising when you think about it. Having put our heart and soul into what we do, naturally we worry about negative judgements. Do not panic! Attending an interview with a portfolio of your work gives you a big advantage. Unlike your contemporaries who rarely get the chance to show what they can do except in exams, not only do you get to show what you are best at – being creative – but you also have plenty of time to prepare in advance, a good idea of what to expect, and all the people interviewing you will be artists themselves so they will understand what you are doing.

## What is a portfolio?

A portfolio is a folder containing examples of art and design work. Professional artists and designers need to take their portfolios to job interviews. You will show your portfolio to the admissions tutors of the courses to which you apply. Portfolios come in all shapes and sizes and in many cases you will be able to use the same one (normally A2 size) in which to display your work for both Foundation and degree applications (though obviously the contents will be different!).

There are some exceptions. For example, a student applying for a specialist degree course in photography might choose to use a portfolio specifically designed for that purpose. They are often smaller and are sometimes referred to as 'books'. In fact, the term 'portfolio' can be used to describe any collection of works for presentation even if they are not actually displayed exclusively in a folder. Some institutions or courses may require the portfolio to be submitted online.

## Which portfolio should you buy?

At this stage, do not buy one at all. Wait until you have read the whole of this book, have had a chance to think things over and, most importantly, have some idea of what you are going to put in it. As a guide, buy the best one that you can afford, as it will protect your work better and be a saving in the long term. Look at the quality of the zip if it has one and check that the ring binder works well. Is the handle strong and comfortable? When thinking about sizes, consider how big your work is. On the other hand, do not bite off more than you can chew. If you cannot carry it, it is too big! Above all, though, remember that it is the quality of your work that counts and not the quality of the thing that you carry it in.

## Getting your work together

The following guidelines apply to portfolios for both Foundation and degree course applications. Read them carefully: they describe the qualities that you should look for in your work and will help you make decisions about which pieces to select. Later in this chapter there are also sections giving guidance on the requirements for each type of portfolio. Make sure you read the contributions made by course tutors.

The first step in putting together your portfolio is to gather together all of your work. When you do this it might be tempting to say 'I won't need that' or 'That's no good', but at this stage just concentrate on getting all of your work in one place so you can see what you have got: finished pieces, unfinished pieces, sketchbooks, models, notebooks, written work, old work, new work – get everything! This is important because not only will you find things that have been tucked away that are actually very good, but also, as you look through your work, you will begin to see relationships emerging between new and old pieces. A small sketch that at first may seem rather unimpressive might have inspired a later, much more accomplished piece. The ability to make judgements and to evaluate what you have done, to recognise a good idea and to develop it further, is an important part of the creative process. Admissions tutors will be assessing to what extent you are able to do these things – they want to see the process, not just the finished work.

It may help you to organise your work into categories. The following list will provide you with a starting point:

- contextual studies/written work
- drawings from observation
- drawings of invention
- finished pieces
- life drawings
- models and maquettes
- sketchbooks/journals
- sketches and studies
- works in progress.

## The importance of drawing

Albert Einstein used the formula $E = mc^2$ to express his famous theory of relativity. Scientists use mathematics to express and explore their understanding of the world and how it works. Artists and designers do this with drawing.

Drawing could usefully be described as the act of making marks to convey meaning. Artists and designers use drawing to record observations, work out ideas, pass on information, express feelings and emotions and resolve practical problems. Drawings are often used to help us visualise how things fit together. For example, scale drawing can be used to work out whether all the units of a kitchen will fit into the space available. Diagrams and flowcharts can be used to demonstrate how ideas and principles relate to each other. Drawings come in all shapes and sizes and are made with a variety of different purposes in mind. Examples of types of drawing include:

- life drawings
- observational drawings, such as those done from a still life or made in the field (e.g. architectural details)
- plans and designs
- sketches and drafts.

Whichever course you apply to, the admissions tutors will want to see your drawings in one form or another because they are evidence of your visual intelligence and thought process. Your drawings demonstrate that you can perceive, understand, invent and communicate visually. These abilities are at the core of successful art making.

## Sketchbooks

Sketchbooks fulfil many purposes. They are a place in which artists and designers begin the creative process. They are also a place in which to store cuttings, postcards and virtually any other articles that will fit. They are the place in which you can put your ideas, thoughts and feelings down on paper. Typically, interesting sketchbooks contain visualisations of many types, made by you for a variety of reasons.

These images might take the form of carefully studied observational drawings or quick sketches or doodles. In a sketchbook you will refer back to previous ideas and make relationships between the images on one page and those on another. Perhaps you have spent some time experimenting with different ways of making marks. You will be familiar with many of the effects that you can get with a pencil, but what kind of drawings could you make with a nail? A sketchbook or journal is the place where you might try something like this. Maybe you have been using your sketchbook to work out the volume of a space so you can calculate how much concrete you would need to fill it? Why would you want to know? At this stage you are probably not completely sure and you do not need to be.

The sketchbook is a place where you can try things out even if they seem crazy; it will reveal the extent of your curiosity. In this sense, sketchbooks can be highly personal and frequently become much cherished. They also provide evidence of your creative development because they are time-based.

With very few exceptions, course admissions tutors will want to see your sketchbook work.

## Project work

Project pieces might be two- or three-dimensional or time-based (such as video) and may use a variety of media. Normally they will have been completed on your current course of study and will show to what extent you have taken advantage of the training and support you have been given.

The ability to undertake and complete a project, whether it is self-determined or in response to a set brief, is one of the qualities that prospective art schools and colleges look for. Work developed over an extended period – formed by experimentation, contemplation, reflection and risk taking – says a great deal about its creator.

- Are you willing to stick with something to the end?
- Will you test a theory to the point of destruction?
- Can you keep an open mind?

A project piece will demonstrate your imagination, invention and skill and give evidence of your willingness to condense your theories and commit to a final outcome. If it has been made as part of a group project it will also show your ability to work with others. It can also be very helpful to include some work in progress in your portfolio. Unfinished pieces can have a freshness and ambiguity that often stimulates conversation.

Overly prepared portfolios in which everything is polished to perfection may come across as stifled and dishonest, and show little of your process; including an unfinished piece or two will help to avoid this problem.

### Personal work

Most artists and designers have a strong desire to be creative. Whether they are extrovert or introvert by nature, creative people have a need to express themselves. Inevitably, this does not stop when you leave the classroom or studio. Personal work may take a variety of forms, but its essential qualities are that you did it because you wanted to, it contains your own opinions, thoughts and feelings, and it was made to fulfil your needs. Maybe you feel strongly about something and want to make a point or perhaps you are in a band, have recorded a demo and need a CD cover. In both cases, you would naturally have a need to create. Personal work says a lot about who you are and demonstrates your passion and commitment.

### Contextual studies/written work

Written work is often overlooked at interview but should be included if possible. At degree level it will be a requirement to complete some form of contextual study, and on a Foundation course you can expect to be fully engaged in critical thinking (although you probably will not be required to produce an extended written piece). Reflecting on the work of others and responding to its qualities are fundamental parts of the creative process. This work will give you the chance to demonstrate your ability to explore ideas and concepts and learn from the work of others and, in many cases, will show how you are able to make choices about typefaces, justifying text and formatting illustrations.

## Matching your portfolio to the course specification

Make sure that you read the course's portfolio specification thoroughly. Talk things through to make sure that you are clear about what is required. Each course will have its own requirements. For example, many courses ask you to limit your portfolio to a particular number of pieces. Whatever the requirements are, respect them; they will be there for a reason and are your best guide to what to include. In many cases it will be necessary for you to adapt your portfolio for each course to which you apply. Make sure that you give yourself time to do this.

### Special considerations

It may not be possible to take all of your work to the interview; perhaps it is too big or too fragile. For practical reasons, art schools and colleges inevitably have to put some restrictions on what can be accepted. If this is the case, in most instances it is perfectly acceptable to take photographs, but do check with the admissions tutors first. Original work is preferable if possible, and if you do take photographs make sure that they are good ones.

> **TIP!**
>
> Label your portfolio – make sure that you clearly identify your work. You do not want there to be any confusion about who did it and you want to make sure that you will get it back. This is particularly important if you have to submit your portfolio in advance of the interview – do put your name and address in an obvious place.

## Digital portfolios

Many institutions accept or even encourage you to submit your portfolio digitally. This could be in one of a number of formats:

- uploading images of your work to a web-based site such as Flickr or YouTube
- submitting your work as a pdf portfolio
- creating your own website or blog in which to showcase your work.

Your chosen institution will give you advice on the number of pieces, the type of work it wants to see, and technical information on the format it wants the work in, and how to upload it or send it.

> **TIP!**
>
> - Ensure that you use digital file sizes that are neither too large (in case they cannot be attached to an email or downloaded easily), nor too small so that the quality of the image is not sufficiently good for a selector to assess your work.
> - If you are photographing your paintings, drawings or 3D pieces, use a good-quality camera and ensure the lighting is good. Avoid shadows, reflections, camera glare or distracting backgrounds.
> - Make sure that everything is labelled clearly: your name, any titles of the works, when they were made and any other information you feel is important. This might include materials you used, techniques or influences.

## Your portfolio

Robert Green, previously Manager of International Student Support at the University of the Arts London, gives advice about portfolios.

*The majority of our courses at the University of the Arts London are studio/practice-focused and as such entry is generally based on portfolio assessment and interview. Therefore, careful preparation and selection of the portfolio is an essential preliminary to the interview.*

*The portfolio is a visual diary. It is the documentation of the individual's journey, both perceptually and conceptually, over a period of time. In essence the portfolio should be comprehensive, demonstrating a breadth and depth of inquiry, curiosity and genuine investigation. Solid practical skills and experience of working with a variety of media and techniques are, in addition, of equal importance.*

*The portfolio should include work done in school or college and at home. The range of approaches and the materials used should show that the applicant has made the most of the opportunities around them, in terms both of what they are being taught and the art room or studio facilities that are available. We particularly look for evidence that an applicant has been prepared to develop some ideas further on their own initiative and in their own time.*

*Time and care are needed in selecting the portfolio, and systematic decisions about what to include and how to organise and present the work should be made. Obvious repetition should be avoided, as should over-selection. A limited number of relevant works in progress may be included because, first and foremost, we are looking for potential.*

*Ideally, a portfolio should consist of between 25 and 50 pieces of recent work, completed over a two-year period. This collection of work should show evidence of a broad-based creativity and include sketchbooks, visual research books, idea sheets and any experiments or explorations in three dimensions. The portfolio should demonstrate, through project and thematically based work, evidence of individual creativity and the development of ideas. Generally, it is important that work reflects and demonstrates creative thinking and a personal commitment to a particular project.*

*In the early stages of all our courses we concentrate on combining technical workshops with set projects. As courses progress, assignments generally become more wide-ranging and contextually based. All practical work is undertaken within a framework of*

> *individual and group tutorials as well as studio criticism sessions, where all students are encouraged to offer constructive critical opinions and advice to each other. Critical exchange and dialogue is central to our teaching approach.*
>
> *Therefore, at interview all applicants are expected to discuss and evaluate the development and context of their work so as to demonstrate broad understanding and an ability to think critically.*
>
> *A portfolio is not a mere supplement to an interview, but is the main factor in assessing a student's future potential. Thus the portfolio is even more essential to students who are unable to be interviewed.*
>
> *You could present your portfolio in the form of colour photographs or colour photocopies. However, most likely, you will be asked to digitise your folder and upload it to a chosen site. You should send between 25 and 50 pieces of work.*
>
> *The University of the Arts London has representatives in a number of countries across the world. Our representatives can assist with all aspects of the application procedure, offer information about programmes and courses and assist with immigration matters.*
>
> *When our senior academics make their next scheduled visit, a local representative can arrange for applicants to have an interview or an advice session with an academic. Our contact details and an overseas schedule can be found on our website.*

## Enrolling on short courses

Short courses can be a valuable source of extra tuition. They give you a taster of what being at art school is like and can be a lot of fun. For mature applicants, they provide the opportunity to work with teachers and become reacquainted with a teaching environment. If you do not have access to a life model, for example, consider taking life-drawing classes. Courses could be theoretical in nature and could cross over into other disciplines that are new to you, for example animation. Not only will this help to build up your portfolio, but it will also be an excellent demonstration of your commitment.

Taking a short course at a university you are considering attending is a good way of expressing your interest, and you may even meet and build a relationship with the admissions tutors. Some institutions, such as the University of the Arts London, offer portfolio preparation short courses.

## Portfolio reviews

Many schools and colleges offer portfolio review sessions, sometimes leading up to mock interviews. Certainly your teacher or tutor will offer you advice and support. Remember, you are not always the best judge of what to put in and what to leave out of your portfolio. You are going to need a second opinion, and taking the advice of an experienced teacher will help enormously.

## Freak-outs

Most artists feel overwhelmed from time to time – it often goes with the territory for those of us who are willing to test things to the limit. The process of putting together a portfolio can feel stressful at the best of times, and if you leave everything to the last minute it will be even worse. You also need to make sure you leave time to think about what you are going to say at interview.

When a group of A level students applying to art school were asked 'If you could give a fellow art school applicant one piece of advice on how to put together a portfolio, what would it be?', their unanimous response – which they all shouted out – was 'Start early!' Setting manageable weekly deadlines and keeping an honest record of what you have and have not done will help enormously. Set specific goals such as 'I need more life drawing'. Not convinced? Read on.

> *'The other students seemed so confident, so cool, and were carrying so much work. I felt very intimidated. But the interview itself was much less stressful than I had thought. The interviewer asked me to choose one piece from my portfolio and explain its story – where I got the idea (from an exhibition I had been to), what preliminary work I did (I showed him some sketches and colour swatches in my notebook) and how I would develop the idea (I hadn't thought about this but talked a bit about incorporating some collage into it next time). He smiled and encouraged me all the time. And I was offered a place!'*
>
> Pat

> *'I had two interviews for Foundation courses, at UAL and Kingston. The thing that they had in common was that the atmosphere was very relaxed in both interviews, more like a chat about my likes and future plans. The interviewers seemed interested in my portfolio work and allowed me to talk about the pieces I liked best, prompting me with questions about ideas for future development of the pieces, or where I got the ideas from. The difference was that for one of the interviews, the university had run a workshop at my*

college a month before, on how to prepare for their interviews, so I not only knew what to expect but I had also met my interviewer before. So I went in feeling confident. At the other interview, I had three people in the room asking me questions so I was much more nervous. My advice for students applying is to find out as much as you can about the interview process in advance by talking to current students – ask your school for the names of previous students who have gone to the university.'

*Charlotte*

'To be honest, I really enjoyed the portfolio preparation process for my Foundation course. I was quite nervous the day before the interview, but practising and becoming more confident in talking about my work definitely helped. It was important to stay focused and try to remain calm. Going through my portfolio and double-checking that everything is in order was a good way to occupy myself and ensure I was prepared before my interview.

'I was lucky enough to get feedback and support from my teachers, and that was crucial in preparing for portfolio reviews and interviews. They offered me valuable advice on how to present my work effectively and discuss my creative process. Additionally, my tutors organised portfolio review sessions and mock interviews to provide further guidance and prepare me for the actual interview process.

'I found discussing my work in front of strangers helped me to become more comfortable with articulating my ideas, showcasing my passion, and demonstrating my artistic development. Talking openly and confidently about my artwork and my aspirations for the future made a positive impression on the real interviewers.'

*Julia*

'I hadn't been given much advice from my previous school about applying for art courses, and didn't realise that I needed to do Foundation. I just assumed that I would apply for the fashion degree I wanted to follow. My portfolio was full of fashion sketches but not much else. My UCAS applications were rejected without interview but one college did contact me and asked me to come to a Foundation interview. They were very nice but didn't offer me a place because my portfolio "showed no real variety or evidence of research". They advised me to take another year of A level and to do textiles and photography in a year and also get help on my portfolio. I was annoyed at first, but in fact the extra year taught me so much about finding sources of ideas and developing them into something personal. I got offers from all of my chosen Foundation courses, and ended up here at UAL. My advice – research courses and their requirements.'

*Billy*

> 'Make sure you get someone to help you to practise before the real interview. Not to rehearse as if you were in a play, but by asking you questions about your work; ideas; future plans. I was lucky because my school organised practice interviews and portfolio crit sessions but I met some people at the interview who were very, very nervous because they had no idea what to expect.'
>
> Libby

## Foundation course portfolios

Your Foundation course portfolio should contain as wide a variety of work as possible. You may think that you are heading for a career in fashion design, but you are applying for a diagnostic course that aims to confirm that choice for you or point you in another direction. Tutors want to see potential in all sorts of areas, so include:

- colour work made in a variety of media
- contextual studies or written work
- drawings and paintings made from observation and imagination, using a variety of media
- examples of design work and model-making
- life drawings
- multimedia work such as video
- photography
- photographs of three-dimensional work if it is not possible to transport it
- printmaking
- project work made on your current course and for yourself
- sketchbooks.

Don't worry if you cannot include all of these; very few students are able to. Remember that admissions tutors will primarily be looking for potential and motivation.

---

### What ECA admissions tutors look for in a portfolio

Birgitta MacDonald, Director of First Year Studies (Art and Design General Course) at Edinburgh College of Art (ECA), has the following advice about your portfolio.

*The portfolio tells us about you. It tells us what art and design experience you have had and what kind of course you have followed. It tells us about your imaginative and creative responses to ideas, to observations, to process and to concepts. The portfolio will be* looked at to assess the individual candidate's enthusiasm, creativity, intellectual and practical skills in the practice of art and design.

Consideration will be given to the candidate's potential for further development and progress in any of the fields of art and design the college has to offer. The admissions panels will also be looking for signs of the following student attributes:

- strong portfolio displaying research, visual and manipulative skills based on the portfolio grading system used in First Year Studies at ECA
- a willingness to broaden the existing skill base and to be fully committed to a broad, general, diagnostic first-year course, leading to specialist study in the second year
- good communication skills – visual, verbal and written
- an inquisitive nature and an ability to demonstrate intellectual curiosity
- self-motivation and drive
- organisational skills (timekeeping, presentation of folio, etc.).

The portfolio should include representative examples of work undertaken as part of a programme of study and/or personal research. The compilation of a portfolio should not be regarded as an end in itself, but rather as one of the results of that study.

The portfolio is the primary means by which a candidate presents herself/himself to the admissions panels and it should be prepared accordingly. Logical presentation assists in this and there is much to be gained by grouping work in categories such as drawing, painting, two-dimensional design and so on, in chronological order. It is also valuable to be able to trace the development of a work and preliminary studies are best presented with the final work.

There should be evidence of study and investigation, the exploration in depth or in breadth of a subject/interest in a sustained way. Portfolios should display, in some form, evidence of developing skills relevant to artistic practice – for example drawing skills, colour investigation, making skills, photographic skills. Alongside these there should be evidence of a lively interest in the collection of relevant research materials such as photographs, magazine articles, historical data, collected objects and personal notes. The admissions panels will pay particular attention to candidates' notebooks/sketchbooks, especially with regard to the extent to which they reflect the range of a candidate's interests and experience.

## Specialist course portfolios

While this portfolio should contain a range of work demonstrating your all-round ability, you will obviously need to demonstrate a commitment to a particular area of study and show a level of skill and ability in that field. However, admissions tutors will be realistic about the extent to which you will have been able to develop your skills and will very much be looking for potential and motivation. Items to include are:

- colour work made in a variety of media
- contextual studies or written work
- drawings made from observation and imagination, using a variety of media
- life drawings
- personal work in your specialisation made for yourself
- photography
- photographs of three-dimensional work as required, if it is not possible to transport it
- project work in your specialised area of study made on your current course
- sketchbooks.

With respect to your specialist project work, use the following examples as a starting point for ideas on what to include. As a rule, your portfolio should contain a sustained project made within your proposed area of study. Contact the course admissions tutors if you are unsure about what to put in.

### Fashion

Drawings, sketches and collages showing design development; final designs; toiles; photographs or actual examples of garments you have made; a collection of information on particular designers, fashion manufacturers or shops; a design project worked on to a brief; evidence that you read fashion magazines and follow developments on the catwalk.

### Film, TV and animation

A short film that you may have made as part of a course project; scripts; storyboards; a subject-dedicated sketchbook; drawings; photography; evidence that you regularly watch films and read reviews.

## Fine art

Paintings and/or sculptures, photographs, textiles and pieces of work produced to a negotiated brief; original pieces, produced entirely from your own ideas; evidence that you read art magazines and visit exhibitions.

## Graphic design

Lettering; samples of freehand drawing; examples of work showing page layout; projects relating to advertising, publicity or packaging; typography; work completed to a brief, such as a complete publicity campaign for a product; digitally manipulated images; evidence that you read design magazines and visit exhibitions.

## Illustration

Work done from direct observation; work related to a design and technology project (if applying for technical or scientific illustration courses); work done to a brief – for example, a piece done to illustrate pages of a particular book, with sample text and notes explaining how you set out to emphasise particular aspects; evidence that you read appropriate literature and visit exhibitions.

## Product design

Drawings, diagrams, computer-aided designs; working notes showing that you understand the workshop processes necessary to manufacture the product; preliminary sketches; photographs of the finished article; evidence that you read design magazines and visit exhibitions.

## Guidance on portfolio preparation for specialist courses

> 'Interviews are an opportunity for you to demonstrate your commitment and self-motivation to a chosen area of study, and to discuss aspects of your chosen course and ask any questions that you may have. You will be expected to display and discuss your portfolio. Portfolios should contain examples of work (both finished and in progress) that showcase your particular interests – not only course or school work, but also any independent work, including, for example, sketchbooks and any other evidence of your ideas, your interests and passion for your chosen area of study.

> 'The form of portfolio work desired would vary according to the area of study. For example, the BA (Hons) in Costume course would require extensive evidence of figurative drawing whereas the BA (Hons) in Model-making would require that you show items that

you have made, whether in pottery, wood or fabric. The common requirement across the board of courses is that you show evidence of your commitment to your area of study and an ability to visually express your ideas and concepts and show the creative development of your artwork from start to finish. The creative process is an important feature rather than the outcome. Passion for your chosen area of study is also essential as well as the ability to demonstrate and show your potential within a variety of artwork pieces.'

*Astrid MacKellar, Arts University Bournemouth*

## The skills your portfolio should demonstrate

- **Drawing:** evidence of life drawing can be useful because it demonstrates such a particular discipline, but any drawing that shows you can observe and interpret the world around you is important. Drawings can be any scale and in any medium, but a diversity of approaches shows exploration and a keenness to experiment.
- **Problem-solving:** your ability to solve visual problems can be demonstrated through design sheets or sketchbooks, but should show in detail how you would deal with design briefs or your own (if more fine art-based) issues or ideas. If anything, these are the most revealing parts of the interview, and for many staff it is more important than seeing finished pieces.
- **Diversity:** a diversity of work and a willingness to experiment are crucial. A good problem-solver needs to use any number of techniques and approaches, so you must show flexibility and adaptability. If you come with only one method of working, your methods will look narrow and limited.
- **Consistency:** as well as diversity, you need to show that you can also take an idea and 'run with it'; that you have developed, in some depth, one or more particular projects or themes.
- **Independence:** at degree level you will need to be able to generate work that is self-directed and independent. Your portfolio, therefore, needs to show that you have developed your own ways of working that haven't been directed solely by your tutors.
- **Critical/contextual studies:** most degree courses have a theoretical element, usually involving written work, so something that shows your ability to write is also important. Interviewers will also need to know that you are interested in the broader context of art and design. You will be asked about practitioners who have influenced or impressed you and exhibitions you've recently visited.

'Finally, it is impossible to quantify the amount and type of work to take to an interview. While you should include a full range of work that isn't over-edited, you should select carefully rather than include *absolutely everything you've ever made! Emphasise your most recent work as this is the work that best represents your current concerns. Because it is fresh in your mind this is also the work you'll be able to talk about with the most enthusiasm.*

*'The key to your portfolio is its organisation. Have a strong beginning and end, and order your work coherently in projects or subjects, giving most emphasis to recent work. Listen to advice from tutors: they have great expertise in helping students gain university places. For three-dimensional or large-scale work, bring good-quality photographs or slides. Better still, bring originals, but good reproductions will often suffice.'*

Sarah Horton, BA (Hons) Course Leader at<br>Norwich University College of Art

*'Ideally, we would like to see a portfolio that demonstrates a high level of visual skill, creativity, commitment and self-motivation. We would be looking for evidence of intellectual enquiry and cultural awareness. We would expect you to have completed a Foundation course and the resulting portfolio may include sketchbooks, ideas books, set projects, self-initiated work, finished pieces, work in progress, photographs or three-dimensional work.*

*'We value a portfolio of work that includes continuity of ideas, and a series of related images that relate to each other in some way. We are interested in your research, thinking and projects that show the development and progression of an idea. We particularly value self-initiated work because it tells us so much about you! Your portfolio should be self-explanatory – it may be viewed initially in your absence. Edit your work and play with the sequencing of images and projects until they unfold in such a way that they tell us who you are and what you think. And, above all, we are looking for potential.'*

Debbie Cook, Tutor at the Royal College of Art and<br>International Postgraduate Coordinator at Central Saint Martins

*'A portfolio should speak for itself and tell us about your ideas, your passions and your personal approach to working. A commitment to the subject and an engagement with projects should be evident. You need to be self-motivated and have the capacity to work independently and this should be reflected in your portfolio. We are interested in the journey your work takes, your ability to recognise and generate ideas, explore their possibilities and develop them. This process of thinking and working, within a broad cultural context, is crucial. Finally, present your work in a clear and organised way to ensure that it communicates all that you want it to.'*

Annette Bellwood, International Academic Coordinator,<br>London College of Communication

> **WARNING!**
> On no account even consider 'borrowing' someone else's work for your portfolio. As well as being unethical, you are almost certain to be found out, as the differences of style will be quite obvious to the trained eyes of the interviewers.

## Checklist

- Round up your work.
- Check out courses' portfolio specifications.
- Purchase a portfolio.
- Enrol on short courses.
- Review your portfolio.
- Set targets and deadlines.
- Photograph three-dimensional work.
- Label your portfolio.
- Adapt your portfolio to a particular specification.

# 8 | The interview

This chapter is about how to make the most of your interview. Although the format of the interview will vary from college to college and there are differences between interviewing for a Foundation course and a specialist degree course, the following guidelines will be of help to you. Make sure that you read this chapter in conjunction with Chapter 7.

## What is the purpose of the interview?

Interviews are there to help art schools find the most appropriate students and to help students find the most appropriate art schools. Most people who fear interviews do so either because they misunderstand their purpose or because they do not know what to expect and imagine the worst. We worry that we will be asked impossible questions, that the interviewers will not like us or that they will try to catch us out; we worry that we will not be good enough.

Consider this: art schools exist because students want to study art and design. Without the students there would be no colleges, no lecturers, no admissions tutors and no courses. In other words, where would art schools be without you? You are the single most important element in the educational process and, as such, it is not in any college's interest to make life difficult for you. Yes, interviewers will be trying to find out whether you are suited to the course for which you are applying and, yes, they will be carefully considering both you and your work and, yes, you can expect to be asked some challenging questions – but try to take a positive attitude. Most people are nervous at interview; admissions tutors understand this and will make allowances. They are there to get the best from you.

Also, remember that the interview provides you with an opportunity to assess a prospective college. Hopefully, you will have visited the college before your interview and checked things out, but a second look around will not do you any harm. Since you will probably be studying under some of the people who will be interviewing you, check them out too.

## What to expect

The process for interviewing depends on the course and institution you are applying to. In some cases, you may not be interviewed at all; in others you will deliver your portfolio for consideration prior to being offered an interview; and at others, you leave your portfolio with the admissions tutors on the day of your interview, they initially look at it without you and then ask you in to discuss it with them – this may be 10 minutes after they take it or sometime later that day.

In many instances, especially at interviews for degree courses, the interview begins with you being asked to present your work briefly to an interviewer or a panel of interviewers who are seeing it for the first time. As you show your work, the conversation will develop into a more formal question-and-answer session. Some institutions, especially those that request the submission of a portfolio online, conduct interviews through an online video call. As interviews vary from college to college, it is best to read the college's literature to try to find out as much as you can about their particular process before attending.

Interviews vary in length from as little as five or 10 minutes to up to 30 or 40 minutes for specialist degree courses. Do not be surprised or worried if the interview feels as if it was very short. Time seems to pass much more rapidly in this kind of situation. Also remember that the interviewers are experts, know what they are looking for and often will be able to come to a decision quickly. This is particularly the case for Foundation courses, where admissions tutors will frequently have to see literally hundreds of students in a matter of weeks.

In some cases you will find out if you have been successful on the day, but in most cases you will be notified by letter in due course.

## Preparing

It is impossible to know exactly what you will be asked at interview, and in some ways it is not helpful to be overly prepared since it is much better to allow a discussion to develop naturally, answering the questions that you have been asked rather than insisting that you talk about what you have been reading up on. However, while being over-prepared is one thing, being under-prepared is quite another and should be avoided at all costs – it will suggest to the interviewers that you are not really interested in the course. The best way to prepare is to think in general about how you might respond to the specific questions you know that you are likely to be asked. As a guide, consider the following.

- Why have you applied for this particular course?
- Why have you applied to study it here?
- Which artists have influenced you?
- What are you hoping to do in the future?

If you have been conscientious about choosing a course, you will be able to make a positive response to the first two questions. (Make sure that you have read Chapters 2 and 3.) Rereading your notes and personal statement, looking through the course prospectus and talking things through with others will all help. Rather than trying to 'revise' for the answers that you think the interviewers will want, simply remind yourself of what you have done, so that you can respond honestly.

With respect to the question 'Which artists have influenced you?', before going to the interview look through your work and consider how it relates to that of others. If you have worked on a written project, reread it. Looking through your sketchbooks and scrapbooks can also help, since they are, in part, a record of your creative process. These visual prompts will help to remind you of your influences.

During the period leading up to your interview, make a point of getting out and about. Make sure that you visit some exhibitions. In addition to looking at well-known exhibits in museums, go and see a show of new work. Also, keep up to date by reading the arts pages of national newspapers and periodicals – see the reading list in Chapter 12.

If you are applying for a place on a Foundation course it is likely that your future plans will include taking a degree. You can say this. If you are applying for a place on a specialist degree course, jotting down a few notes to help you think things through may be helpful in preparing for the fourth question, the one about your future plans. Whatever your thoughts might be, do not worry if you cannot come up with a complete answer. That is perfectly normal. It would be a pretty boring world to live in if we all knew exactly what we were going to do in the future! You just need to be able to show the interviewer that you are reflecting on your options and have some possible ideas in mind.

Assuming that you have done your homework and know as much as possible about the course, you will not need to use up valuable time asking questions about course structure or discussing specific issues such as funding. If you are given the chance to ask questions or make comments, it is usually much better to respond to something you have just been discussing with the interviewer than to set your own agenda.

Perhaps the best way to prepare for this is by taking a mock interview, which will give you a feel for how an interview develops. Many schools and colleges offer mock interviews to their own students and in some cases to external candidates. If you have the chance to do one, make sure you do not miss out. Mock interviews provide excellent preparation and an excellent way to identify and resolve potential problems.

Discussing your work with art college or university teachers can be a daunting prospect and you will need to practise before your interview. As a general rule of thumb, try to structure any discussion of your work as follows.

1. Where the idea for the piece came from. This is an opportunity to talk about artists whose work you like, exhibitions you have visited or previous work that you have produced.
2. How your ideas were realised in the piece. You could talk about the composition, the materials and the techniques you used as well as what the work represents.
3. Where the work will lead you. You could talk about what you will work on next, what you might have done differently or how the piece has led you to investigate other artists or techniques.

The interviewer will help you by asking questions and possibly suggesting other areas of research.

## Practicalities

As well as thinking about the kind of questions that you might be asked, it is also important to consider a few practicalities. For example, how will you be travelling to the interview? If you are applying to a local art school you may only have to make a short journey. On the other hand, you may be applying to a course a long way from home, so consider the logistics. In some cases an overnight stay may be necessary.

Also think about how you intend to transport your work. In many instances you will be able to carry everything in a portfolio. As has been mentioned, most colleges are happy to look at photographs of three-dimensional or larger pieces. However, in some situations (e.g. with pieces under a certain size) it will be necessary to take this work with you. You may need to ask a friend for help or to ask the college for advice. Can you comfortably manage your portfolio or is it too heavy?

Practise your presentation technique. Whether you are an international or Home student, your interview may be via an online video call. If your interview is going to be done remotely, make sure you have a good internet connection and that your webcam is of good enough resolution to show your work properly.

## The night before

Assuming that you are well organised, there should be nothing left to do except relax and get a good night's sleep, so make sure that you do! Easy to say, difficult to do. We all get nervous before a big day and you might find it difficult to switch off. Don't worry if this happens – it just means that you're normal. Try doing something to take your mind off things, like watching a film, chatting with friends or maybe taking a little gentle exercise, and try not to worry. Be positive. Remember, art schools cannot exist without students!

## The interview itself: some tips

- Make sure you arrive early. You do not want to be rushing around at the last minute.
- Dress comfortably. Your interviewers will be far more interested in who you are and what you do than what you wear. If your hair is bright blue and shaved on one side, fine. If it is not, well that's fine too. You will need much more than a good hairstyle to get into art school!
- Make eye contact. If you are asked to show your work, don't turn your back on the interviewers; try to position your portfolio between yourself and the people you are speaking to, or, if you are standing side by side, turn towards them from time to time.
- Be willing to listen as well as talk. Sometimes when we are nervous we talk too much. Try to listen carefully to the questions that you are being asked. You will respond far more intelligently if you understand what has been said. If you do not understand, do not be afraid to ask for further explanation. Sometimes there will be pauses in the conversation. Do not let this unnerve you: the tutors are just concentrating while they look at your work.
- Understand *why* you have been asked to attend an interview. It is because what the university knows about you so far (what you have written in your personal statement, your work that you have submitted in an online application your academic history or what your teachers have written about you) leads them to believe that you would be a valuable presence at the university or art school, and that you have the potential to become a successful artist, designer or architect. So be confident!
- Be willing to consider new ideas. You will be very difficult to teach if you find it hard to keep an open mind. Try not to become defensive if some of your responses to questions are challenged.
- Try and relax before you walk in, and then be natural, authentic and believe in yourself.
- Remember to switch your phone off, or on silent. You don't want it distracting you or the interviewer.
- Be yourself. You do not need to put on an act. Never try to bluff or lie. You will always be found out, so only show your own work and if you do not know something then say so.
- Above all, be enthusiastic. Do not be afraid to express your commitment and passion for your subject. You will have worked very hard up to this point. Let your interviewers know that this matters to you. Try not to be cool. Art schools are looking for motivated students.

> **HOPE**
>
> Use the acronym HOPE as a reminder of the personal qualities that you will try to display at interview:
>
> - honesty
> - open-mindedness
> - preparedness
> - enthusiasm.

Meet up with a friend and talk things through; this will help you to put things into perspective. Also it will greatly help your fellow students if you give them some feedback. They may not have had an interview yet and your experience will be beneficial. A day or two later, when you have had the chance to reflect a little, make a note of anything that sticks in your mind that might be helpful for next time.

> 'Before my interview for the Fine Art Photography BA at the Glasgow School of Art, I was thinking about all the different questions they might ask; but when it came to it, it was quite straightforward and they didn't try to catch me out. They asked me to talk about three influences on my work and why the course would suit me, but mostly the interview was about my work. I chose the Glasgow course because the darkroom was very impressive and I could see myself working well there. They asked me about this and the darkroom techniques I was using in my work. I think the interview went well because I could show that I had some intentions going into the course and that I was eager to be proactive.'
>
> Lucy Mullican, BA Fine Art Photography, Glasgow School of Art

> 'I had one interview for a Foundation course and two for BA Textiles, all of which were successful. The advice I would give you is: be well-prepared, practise interview skills and seek guidance from teachers and tutors. Doing this can significantly improve the chances of success during the portfolio review and interview process. Remember to showcase your passion, creativity and unique artistic perspective.

> 'Building confidence in discussing your work is important and can greatly benefit your interview performance. Ensure that you are familiar with every piece in your portfolio, including the concept, technique and inspiration behind each artwork. Be prepared to discuss why you chose specific pieces, how they showcase your skills and artistic development, and what they mean to you personally.

> 'During interviews, it's not just about the final artwork; interviewers are often interested in understanding your creative process. Be ready to explain the steps you took to create your artwork, from

initial ideation to execution. Discuss the materials, techniques, and concepts you explored and how they influenced your artistic decisions.

'Be open-minded and receptive to feedback, as it shows your willingness to grow and learn from others. Additionally, reflect on your own artistic journey, acknowledging areas where you want to improve and how the chosen course or future studies can support your growth.

'Practise talking about your artwork in front of different audiences, such as friends, family members or fellow artists. This will help you refine your explanations and become comfortable conveying your artistic vision. Remember to stay authentic, passionate and enthusiastic during your interviews.'

Anna Roberts, Foundation, University of the Arts London

'My preparation for my fashion degree course interview at Bristol UWE included designing a little booklet about the university, to show that I was interested in the university as well as the art campus and course. I knew they would ask me about a designer I liked, so I chose someone not so well known, as I thought everyone else would go mainstream. I made sure that my portfolio included things other than fashion as well. I was asked why I chose Bristol, and lots of questions about my portfolio such as "Why did you do the stitching like that?" I was very relaxed at the interview because I made a point of being sociable with the other students who were also waiting to be interviewed.

'Even though the degree was a fashion course, I still had to do other things in years 1 and 2, such as textiles. It was only in the third year that I could steer the degree more to my own interests. Preparing my final collection was exhausting and I would fall asleep within seconds of lying down. We were given two hours a week with teachers and pattern cutters but the rest was all down to me. Money was also an issue as we had to buy all of our own materials. The department chose who would show their work, so although the atmosphere was competitive, we still had to cooperate and get on with each other.'

Annabel Knowles, BA Fashion

## Admissions tutors' advice for interviews

- 'In interviews, the reviewers are looking for students who demonstrate curiosity about why the world looks like it does.'
- 'I will expect them to talk about books, journals and shows, and to be able to get under the skin of a subject.'

- *'Make sure you convince your interviewers that you are passionate about the subject and the particular course you are being interviewed for.'*
- *'When I meet prospective students, I am looking for potential.'*
- *'If you are closed to new ideas it will be impossible to teach you and your place will be offered to someone else.'*
- *'Interview questions focus on both how and why the work [in the portfolio] was produced and how it might develop.'*
- *'I am not interested in technique – technique can be learned – I am interested in ideas and an open mind.'*
- *'If the student I am interviewing hasn't been to see any exhibitions or shows recently, I tend to doubt their real interest in studying art.'*
- *'Your interviewers are looking for creativity and a willingness to experiment.'*
- *'The internet means that no one, however far from a city, has any excuse not to explore new ideas and get inspiration from practising artists.'*
- *'Be as chatty as you can in your interview. We are looking for good communicators who will share their ideas and not be afraid to discuss their own work.'*
- *'We want to make sure that you are energetic, excited about your future studies and, above all, curious.'*

## Checklist

- Visit exhibitions.
- Try to see the work of graduates from the art school, either at degree shows or online.
- Practise talking about your own work.
- Read the arts pages of national newspapers and magazines.
- Review your portfolio.
- Conduct a mock interview.
- Check the interview date, time and location.
- Find out how to get to your interview.

# 9 | Offers and what to do on results day

If you are lucky and receive an offer from a college or university, what do you do then? And if your offer depends on pending examination results, what happens when you receive the results? It depends on the type of course and the type of offer. The options are summarised below.

## Foundation courses

In most cases you will receive an unconditional offer. In other words, the college has been convinced by your portfolio and interview, and it wants you. All you have to do then is to decide whether you want it! However, please note that in nearly all cases you will be expected to complete your current programme of study successfully.

If applicants are rejected for Foundation courses, in most cases it's because their portfolios are not strong enough. Under these circumstances it is often possible to reapply once the portfolio has been strengthened.

### Conditional offers

Under some circumstances you might receive a conditional offer. This normally happens if the college feels that while your work is promising you are not yet ready to cope with the demands of a Foundation course, or because it requires a particular A level grade or, as an overseas student, you would benefit from help with your language skills or with adapting to UK teaching methods in general. In this situation you may be asked to attend a summer course. (There is a charge for these courses.)

### Accepting an offer

Since there is no centralised system for Foundation course applications (other than local schemes such as that run by the University of the Arts London), it is possible to hold a number of offers simultaneously. In this situation, the best strategy is to keep things simple, and not to try to juggle too many balls at one time. When you applied, you had probably already decided which college was your first choice, which was second, and so on. If you are lucky enough to get offers from a number of colleges, stick to your original plan and accept the offer from the place where you most want to study. Do not accept offers from everyone just to keep your options open. Talk to your teachers or careers advisers if you are unsure about your best course of action.

### What if you are rejected?

If you receive rejections, the first thing to do is to get feedback from the institution. If they reject you it is because they are not completely convinced that studying with them is the best option for you. This may be because they feel that your talents would be better directed towards a different course, discipline or environment. It might be because they think that you are not yet ready (creatively, technically or because of your age) to cope with their course. Once you understand why they are not able to offer you a place, you can focus on alternatives or aim to strengthen the areas that they were concerned about and then reapply. Remember that it is not the 'institution' that is rejecting you, it is someone with a creative or academic background who is looking to allocate the places on the course to the students who, in his or her opinion, would be most suited to that course. If you are rejected and have asked for feedback, then you have a number of options open to you.

- Accept one of the other offers that you may have.
- Make new applications to other art schools.
- Take on board their feedback and reapply once you have addressed their concerns. For example, enrol on some short courses or evening classes, or follow a one-year A level/pre-Foundation course.

## Degree courses

You may receive an offer directly from the art school to which you have applied or, if you are applying through UCAS, you will (if all goes to plan) receive offers from more than one college. If you are lucky, these will be unconditional offers (this means that the offer does not depend on your achieving specific grades).

### Conditional offers

If you receive a conditional offer, it will specify what the college requires of you – for instance, it may ask for a good grade in A level Art or, more commonly, good grades in other subjects, particularly if you are going to study for a joint honours degree.

## Accepting an offer

When you have received replies from all of your five choices, you will (if you are lucky) be faced with a choice of institutions or courses. You will have to decide which course you want to hold as your firm choice (either conditional, CF, or unconditional, UF) and which you want as your insurance offer (either conditional, CI, or unconditional, UI). The insurance offer is usually a course that requires lower grades or marks than the firm choice. Once you have heard from all five choices, UCAS will send you a summary of their responses and give you a deadline (usually of about one month) in which to make the choice of the firm and insurance offers.

## Clearing and Extra

If you are unsuccessful, either because you are not made any offers, or because you don't meet the conditions of your conditional offers, you are eligible to enter Clearing. The Clearing period begins in July, and enables you to contact other colleges and make new applications.

There is also a system called Extra. This runs from late February to early July, and allows candidates who are not holding any offers to approach other art schools.

For details of both Clearing and Extra, look at the UCAS website.

# Results day

If your offer for a place on a degree course depends on examination results (such as A levels, Scottish Highers or International Baccalaureate), then the day your results are issued can be a potentially stressful time. Even if you are confident that you have achieved the grades or scores that you need (and it is often easier for students studying art or design to have an idea of how they have done, since a proportion of the work for these subjects is marked internally by the school or college – but be warned: the marks your teachers submit to the examination boards can be moderated up or down), doing some preparation ahead of results day will make the whole experience less nerve-racking.

## Preparation

- Have your UCAS candidate number and a copy of your UCAS form to hand.
- Make sure that you have uninterrupted access to the internet so that you can look at Clearing vacancies on the UCAS website.
- Make sure that your mobile phone is fully charged and you have topped up your credit, in case you need to call universities (you may have to call numerous times).

## Summary of what to do on results day

### *You have the grades or scores that satisfy your conditional offer*

Celebrate! The university will contact you over the following days to confirm your place and give you more information about practical details, for example when to arrive, what to bring, etc.

### *You have narrowly missed your offer*

Log on to your UCAS account, as you may still have been given your place; or you may have a place with your insurance choice. If in doubt, call the universities.

### *You have missed your offers, and this has been confirmed on UCAS Hub*

Use the Clearing lists to investigate other options. Call the universities' advertised Clearing hotlines and give them your UCAS number and the grades/scores that you achieved.

### *What to do if you do better than expected*

If you are holding an offer and have achieved grades significantly better than you needed, then you can decline your offer and use Clearing to pursue other offers. More information can be found at www.ucas.com/undergraduate/clearing-and-results-day/results-day/declining-your-firm-place.

### *What to do if you do not get an offer*

Four words: do not give up.

There are many options open to you. For degree applications, there are the Clearing and Extra systems (see above and www.ucas.com). For Foundation courses, you have the option of making direct contact with other colleges. You should also contact the colleges that rejected you to try to get their advice. It may be that they spotted a weakness in a particular area of your work and might be able to give you guidance on how to remedy this. If you can convince them that you desperately want to come to them and that you will work on that area – by taking evening classes, for example – they might allow you to bring in your updated portfolio later on in the year for reassessment.

If all else fails, you could consider taking a gap year during which you could work on your portfolio to strengthen it. Many colleges offer portfolio courses specifically for this purpose. These are generally part-time and can be on a one-to-one basis, in small groups or online. In some cases, students are recommended to take a new A level (for example, in photography or textiles) and study this on a one-year part-time course, while using their spare time to gain work experience or to enrol on shorter courses that concentrate on, say, life drawing.

# 10 | Fees and funding

If you are planning on studying at a college or university, you need to think about what it will cost you to do so. For some further education courses, UK students who are below an age threshold will not have to pay tuition fees, but in almost all circumstances you will need to pay for higher education and postgraduate courses.

## UK (Home) students

### Foundation courses

Foundation courses are classed as further education courses, rather than higher education. For this reason, student loans are not available. However, students from the UK who are under 19 years old on 31 August in the year that the course starts are eligible for free tuition. Students who do not come into this category may have to pay tuition fees, which are likely to be about £1,000–£8,000 per year depending on where you study.

### Degree and HND courses

The tuition fee that you will have to pay for undergraduate courses will depend on where you live and where you intend to study. Universities are allowed to charge Home undergraduate fees up to £9,250 per year, as part of the government's Teaching Excellence Framework (TEF), which assesses universities and colleges on the quality of their teaching. The tuition fee cap had been set at £9,000 in Wales, but in February 2024 the Welsh government announced that it was increasing to £9,250 for 2024 entry. Elsewhere in the UK, the tuition fee cap has been in place for a number of years and increases are expected in the future.

There are a number of variations between the systems in England, Scotland, Wales and Northern Ireland, which can result in significant differences between the fees that are ultimately paid by students. Currently (for 2024/2025 entry) the rules are as follows, although they may be subject to change in the future.

- Students from England and Wales are required to pay a maximum of £9,250 if they are studying in England, Wales, Scotland or Northern Ireland.
- Students from Scotland who study at Scottish universities are not required to pay tuition fees (or, rather, tuition fees of £1,820 for 2024 entry are covered by the Student Awards Agency for Scotland (SAAS) for students who qualify for Home student status). Scottish students have to pay fees of up to £9,250 if they study in England, Wales or Northern Ireland.
- Students living in Northern Ireland pay up to £4,710 if they attend university in Northern Ireland, up to £9,250 if they study in England, Wales or Scotland.

### EU students

At present, EU students are charged the same fees as charged to non-EU international students, which are significantly higher than those charged to UK students and are determined by each university. Some students from the EU may be eligible for some support in terms of student loans from the UK government, but this is dependent on a number of factors, so it is best to check personal eligibility. Students from the Republic of Ireland are exempt from paying higher fees and are eligible for Home fee status.

## Living expenses

Your living expenses include the cost of your accommodation, food, clothes, travel and equipment, leisure and social activities – plus possible extras like field trips and study visits.

Check university and college websites for information about possible living costs. Some offer more detailed advice than others and give breakdowns under various headings such as accommodation, food and daily travel. Others go even further and give typical weekly, monthly or annual spends.

If you're living away from home, accommodation will make up the largest proportion of your living costs. There is likely to be a range of accommodation options – from a standard room in university halls through to privately rented accommodation – with a range of price points. You'll probably be surprised when you do some research to find that the cheapest and most expensive towns are not as you might have expected; the cost of accommodation often depends on how much of it is available in a particular area.

When choosing accommodation, it is essential to consider its location and factor in the cost of travel to your university or college. It is also important to find out what's included in the accommodation costs (such as utilities, personal property insurance and Wi-Fi) and whether it is possible to pay for accommodation during term time only.

## Funding your studies

How do you fund your time in higher education? Don't ignore this question and leave it until the last minute! You will need to think carefully about how to budget for several years' costs – and you need to know what help you might get from:

- the government
- your family or partner
- paid part-time work
- other sources, such as bursaries and scholarships.

This chapter gives a brief overview of a complicated funding situation, which can vary according to where you come from and where you plan to study. For more details about the different types of funding available and how to apply for them, check your regional student finance website:

- www.gov.uk/contact-student-finance-england
- www.saas.gov.uk
- www.studentfinanceni.co.uk
- www.studentfinancewales.co.uk

### Tuition fee loans

For UK students, tuition fees can be covered by taking out a tuition fee loan, which will be paid directly to your university or college at the start of each year of your course. You are effectively given a loan by the government that you repay through your income tax from the April after you finish your course but only once your earnings reach a certain threshold. Currently, these income thresholds stand at:

- £25,000 per year for students from England
- £27,295 a year for students from Wales
- £27,660 for students from Scotland (who go to university outside of Scotland)
- £22,015 for students from Northern Ireland.

(All figures apply to students starting their course after 1 August 2023.)

So, if you never reach this threshold, you will not have to repay the fees. In addition, any outstanding balance on your loan will be cancelled after a certain period of time if you have not already cleared it in full. The length of time depends on the rules at the time you took out the loan. For students in England who started their studies in September 2023, the repayment period was extended to 40 years (from 30 years), so it is recommended that students in other regions keep a close eye on any developments with respect to the length of the loan repayment period.

The current situation regarding repayments is that you repay 9% of anything you earn over the annual income threshold.

The interest rate charged on student loans depends on what repayment plan you are on, but for students in England who started their course after 1 August 2023 (Plan 5) it is set at the RPI (Retail Price Index) rate of inflation.

## Maintenance loans

In addition to a tuition fee loan, all students can apply for a maintenance or living cost loan. All students are entitled to a maintenance loan; however, the amount you can borrow will be dependent on your household income – in other words, it is means tested. 'Household income' refers to your family's gross annual income (their income before tax). With the exception of loans available to Scottish students, the amount you can claim also varies depending on your living situation, with the maximum loan being available to students living away from home in London.

Each regional student finance website includes a finance calculator tool that will give an estimate of the finance you would be eligible for based on your family income and other factors, and it is well worth looking at this before planning your budget.

### England (2024/2025)

The maximum annual maintenance loan in England:

- £8,610 for those living in the family home
- £10,227 for those living away from home (£13,348 in London).

### Wales (2024/2025)

In Wales, students can get a combination of a maintenance grant, which they do not have to pay back, and a maintenance loan. Although the grants are means tested, most students will get a grant of at least £1,000.

The maximum amounts for maintenance loans and grants in Wales:

- £10,315 for those living in the family home
- £12,150 for those living away from home (£15,170 in London).

### Scotland (2024/2025)

In Scotland, students can get a mix of maintenance loans and non-repayable bursaries (grants) to cover living expenses. These are as follows (all figures per year):

- household income up to £20,999: £2,000 bursary and £9,400 loan
- household income £21,000–£23,999: £1,125 bursary and £9,400 loan
- household income £24,000–£33,999: £500 bursary and £9,400 loan
- household income £34,000 and above: no bursary and £8,400 loan.

Unlike the rest of the UK, household income for Scottish students is measured on the income bands listed above rather than exact household income.

### Northern Ireland (2023/24)

The maximum annual maintenance loan in Northern Ireland:

- £5,250 for those living in the family home
- £6,776 for those living away from home (£9,492 in London).

In addition, you may be eligible for a non-repayable maintenance grant if your household income is below £41,065 and it is paid to you. This is paid alongside any maintenance loan you qualify for and is up to £3,475.

## Postgraduate courses

There are postgraduate loans available to Home students, Irish students and EU students who have been granted settled status. Eligibility criteria and the amounts awarded differ across the regions of the UK, so it is important to check with the student loans organisations of your chosen region to see if you are eligible and how much you might be granted. For example, in England you may be awarded a maximum of £12,167, which is to contribute to tuition fees and living costs. In Wales, the maximum amount is £18,770; this total amount is split between a loan (which has to be repaid) and a household-income dependent grant (which doesn't have to be repaid). In Northern Ireland the maximum amount awarded is £6,500. These are repayable after the end of your course, alongside any student loans for undergraduate study, after you reach an annual income of (as of 2023) £21,000 for students in England and Wales, £27,600 for students in Scotland, and £22,015 in Northern Ireland.

The only exception is the Master of Architecture (MArch). With this course, the postgraduate loan can only be used if you are studying part-time. If you are studying full-time, then you should apply for undergraduate funding. If you are ineligible for undergraduate funding, you can also apply for the postgraduate loan.

Postgraduate students are often self-funded or may be assisted by scholarships from universities or from other organisations. Contacting the institution to which you are applying is a good way to begin exploring your options. See Appendix 1 for telephone numbers, emails and web addresses.

## The Turing Scheme

Following the UK's withdrawal from the European Union, the Erasmus+ scheme has been replaced by the Turing Scheme.

UK educational institutions are able to apply to the Turing Scheme for funding, which they then use to offer educational and training opportunities around the world to students (participating students don't have to be UK nationals). It's worth researching whether an institution you are interested in offers this possibility and what kinds of projects it engages with.

## Other sources of funding

Commercial organisations, charitable trusts, educational institutions and government agencies all offer sponsorship, special grants, access funds and scholarships. If you are facing financial difficulties, a good place to start looking for information is the college to which you are applying. For example, Edinburgh College of Art offers the Andrew Grant Postgraduate Scholarships (worth £10,500) to those studying on postgraduate courses. There are a number of similar sources of support available at institutions throughout the UK. You should look at the funding sections on the institutions' websites for further information. Remember that these scholarships vary in size and availability from year to year, so you should check the websites regularly for updates.

The Arts and Humanities Research Council (AHRC) also offers some funding for art and design students. Contact details can be found in Chapter 12 of this book.

For architecture students, RIBA offers a number of awards and scholarships to students in Part 1 or Part 2 studies (see page 41) and to graduates who are gaining more practical experience. The RIBA Hardship Funds are awarded to students who might not otherwise be able to study architecture or to continue their studies. RIBA also administers postgraduate scholarships, travel scholarships and research scholarships. Details can be found on the RIBA website.

# 11 | Postgraduate courses

Having completed your degree, you can continue your studies, choosing from the wide variety of postgraduate courses that are available. Postgraduate courses allow you either to specialise in a particular field that interests you, or to reach a higher academic level to widen your job opportunities. Applications can be made either in the final year of your degree or after you have graduated and completed a period of professional practice.

## Types of course

When considering whether or not to apply for postgraduate study, your first choices will be between a higher degree, diploma and certificate and between a taught and a research programme. Courses, which vary in structure, include one-, two- and three-year postgraduate degrees, leading, for example, to the award of a Master of Arts (MA), and postgraduate certificates and diplomas that prepare students for specific professions, such as a Postgraduate Certificate in Animation, a Postgraduate Diploma in Museum Studies or a PGCE, the teaching qualification. You will also be able to develop a career in research, with a PhD or MPhil (see below for details) being the starting point.

Postgraduate courses are available at many colleges, art schools and universities. Many institutions offer courses at both undergraduate and postgraduate levels, making it possible to remain within the same institution for all your studies. There are also specialist schools of art such as the Royal College of Art and the Royal Academy Schools of Art which offer only postgraduate courses.

### Master's degrees

Master's courses used to last for one year and the majority were organised as taught programmes. However, there are now numerous two-year courses. It is now also possible to do a master's degree by research – usually leading to a Master of Philosophy (or MPhil). This is a higher-level qualification than an MA but below a doctorate.

Taught master's degrees usually take from nine to 12 months (or two years if you are a part-time student). The first six to nine months are usually studio and classroom based, and are followed by time spent on a research project.

### Doctorates

A Doctor of Philosophy (PhD) is always achieved by research under the guidance of a supervisor – a member of academic staff who shares your interest and is an expert in that particular area. Your area of study will be highly specialised and you will have to submit a thesis – of up to 100,000 words – based on original research. A PhD typically takes four years (but can take longer).

Courses cover the full range of art and design disciplines and, while it is usual to continue working within the same area of study that you have followed at undergraduate level, it is also possible to cross over into other areas.

## Applying for a postgraduate course

There is no centralised system like UCAS for postgraduate courses, nor is there a set closing date. UCAS does have a postgraduate application system, but not all universities are represented. Details can be found on the UCAS website, www.ucas.com/postgraduate/choosing-postgraduate-course. Some taught programmes have deadlines, but it is often possible to begin a research programme at different points during the academic year. There may, in fact, be different starting dates throughout the year for all types of courses – but the autumn term is still the most popular. There is no limit to the number of applications that you may make, but most students make a maximum of six applications and on average around two to three.

Application procedures vary, but in the first instance you should refer to the college at which you intend to study. You will be required to submit a portfolio, attend an interview and, in some cases, present a formal proposal of an intended programme of study. Take a look at the comments below from Andrew Watson to get an idea of how one college approaches the admissions process.

> 'Postgraduate courses have well-defined portfolio requirements. These will vary in relation to the level of postgraduate study (Postgraduate Certificate, Postgraduate Diploma and MA) and in relation to the subject area (design, art, media). Start by checking the published portfolio requirements for the course you are applying to. The portfolio is used as a means of assessing an applicant's

suitability for the level of study and their motivation and potential to achieve the course aims and learning outcomes. At postgraduate level you should be able to demonstrate intelligence and maturity of approach to a personal area of interest as well as confidence in the abilities that you will require to explore a range of technical and formal problems. You should also emphasise your ability to undertake independent research. For design-based studies it is important to show that you can produce, communicate and evaluate a range of ideas and design responses to a particular problem. MA applicants should be able to show critical and analytical abilities and evidence of original thinking. Fine art and media courses would expect the applicant to be able to show, either at interview or in an accompanying statement, an awareness of the cultural and social context of the work submitted in the portfolio.

'Many courses now limit the quantity and form of the work submitted at application and ask for additional examples to be shown at interview. Again, it is very important to check specific published course requirements on this.'

Andrew Watson, Course Director for the
Postgraduate Certificate in Professional Studies in
Art and Design, Central Saint Martins

'My MA in Textiles Mixed Media Design at the Royal College of Art (RCA) allowed me to gain a greater understanding of myself as a creative practitioner. It introduced me to many people from all walks of life who have interests like mine, and these connections have been invaluable.

'I was able to find myself as a practitioner in a highly professional and creative environment, and the college introduced us to well-regarded people from the design industries to help better our work and our understanding of design.

'I took part in a series of competitions while studying at the RCA, and we were offered incredible opportunities to present our work to the public as well as artists, which created a fabtastic platform for from which we could launch our careers.'
Jess Zhao, MA Textiles Mixed Media Design, Royal College of Art

## Advice on choosing and applying for postgraduate courses

- Have a clear idea of what you want to achieve by enrolling on a postgraduate course: are you aiming to develop your practice in a more general way, or are you looking to specialise in a particular area within your chosen field? You will need to decide what you want the outcome to be before choosing which courses to apply for.

- If you are thinking about postgraduate courses because you want to teach within a college or university environment, talk to teachers or lecturers about which courses are most appropriate.
- Many postgraduate students choose their courses because they want to work within a specialised field. For example, by specialising in documentary photography having completed a BA in Photography. Try to find out where graduates from your chosen course end up working, and make sure that your own career plans can be realised by taking the course.
- Talk to the course director before making a final decision to find out what type of students follow the course. Are they recent graduates, or industry professionals looking to extend their skills? Will there be other students with the same experience, qualifications or goals as you?
- Do as much research as you can on who will be teaching you and who will be interviewing you, so that you can tailor your portfolio appropriately.

# 12 | Further information

## Applications

### Degree courses

**UCAS**
Rosehill
New Barn Lane
Cheltenham
GL52 3LZ
Tel: 0371 468 0468
www.ucas.com

**University of Cambridge**
Admissions Office
University of Cambridge
Student Services Centre
New Museums Site
Cambridge
CB2 3PT
Tel: 01223 333308
www.cao.cam.ac.uk

**University of Oxford**
Undergraduate Admissions Office
University Offices
Wellington Square
Oxford
OX1 2JD
Tel: 01865 270000
www.ox.ac.uk

### Books

*HEAP 2025: University Degree Course Offers: The Essential Guide to Winning Your Place at University*, Brian Heap (Trotman)

*How to Complete Your UCAS Application: 2025 Entry*, Ryan Moran & UCAS (Trotman)

## Funding

**UCAS student finance information**
www.ucas.com/ucas/undergraduate/finance-and-support

**Student Loans Company (SLC)**
Tel: 0300 100 0607
www.slc.co.uk

**Arts and Humanities Research Council (AHRC)**
www.ahrc.ac.uk/funding/opportunities/current

## International students

**British Council**
www.britishcouncil.org

**English UK**
www.englishuk.com

**UK Council for International Student Affairs (UKCISA)**
www.ukcisa.org.uk

**International English Language Testing System (IELTS)**
www.ielts.org

**Test of English as a Foreign Language (TOEFL)**
www.ets.org/toefl

## Art and design bodies

### Arts councils

**Arts Council England**
Brooklands
24 Brooklands Avenue
Cambridge
CB2 8BU
www.artscouncil.org.uk

**Arts Council of Wales**
Bute Place
Cardiff
CF10 5AL
https://arts.wales

## 12 Further information

**Arts Council of Northern Ireland**
Linden Hill House
23 Lindenhall Street
Lisburn
BT28 1FJ
www.artscouncil-ni.org

**Creative Scotland**
Waverley Gate
2–4 Waterloo Place
Edinburgh
EH1 3EG
www.creativescotland.com

## Professional bodies

**The Association of Photographers**
Click Studios
Heritage Court
Cherryduck Studios
Sampson St
London
E1W 1NA
www.the-aop.org

**British Film Institute**
Belvedere Road
Lambeth
London
SE1 8XT
www.bfi.org.uk

**Crafts Council**
44a Pentonville Road
London
N1 9BY
www.craftscouncil.org.uk

**Design Council**
Eagle House
167 City Road
London
EC1V 1AW
www.designcouncil.org.uk

**Printmakers Council**
Ground Floor
Unit 23
Blue Anchor Lane
London
SE16 3UL
www.printmakerscouncil.com

## Architecture

**Architects Registration Board**
8 Weymouth Street
London
W1W 5BU
www.arb.org.uk

**Royal Institute of British Architects (RIBA)**
66 Portland Place
London
W1B 1AD
www.architecture.com

**The RIBA President's Medals Student Awards**
www.presidentsmedals.com

## Reading List

The art schools' and universities' websites and brochures often highlight books that they recommend for students. As you will see if you go to online booksellers or visit good bookshops, there are many thousands of books about art, architecture or design. So, where do you start? The following titles are our personal favourites:

*What Are You Looking At?: 150 Years of Modern Art in the Blink of an Eye*, Will Gompertz (Viking)

*Seven Days in the Art World*, Sarah Thornton (Granta Books)

*How to Read Paintings*, Liz Rideal (Bloomsbury Visual Arts)

*The Story of Architecture*, Jonathan Glancey (Dorling Kindersley)

*Modernism*, Richard Weston (Phaidon Press)

*A Cultural History of Fashion in the 20th and 21st Centuries*, Bonnie English (Bloomsbury Academic)

*Photography: A Concise History*, Ian Jeffrey (Thames & Hudson)

*Art Photography Now*, Susan Bright (Thames & Hudson)

*The Pot Book*, Edmund de Waal and Claudia Clare (Phaidon Press)

*The Craftsman*, Richard Sennett (Penguin)

*Graphic Design Visionaries*, Caroline Roberts (Laurence King)

## Magazines

This list only scrapes the surface of the publications available. The best places to look for art and design magazines are museum and gallery bookshops, which carry wide selections.

*Architects' Journal*
*Architectural Review*
*Art Monthly*
*Artist Portfolio Magazine*
*ArtReview*
*B&W* (photography)
*Blueprint* (design)
*British Journal of Photography*
*Ceramic Review*
*Ceramics Monthly*
*Computer Arts Magazine*
*Creative Review*
*Frieze*
*IMA Magazine* (Photography)
*Modern Painters*
*Next Level*
*Photography Monthly*
*TATE ETC.*

## Websites

The internet's shifting landscape means that new sites devoted to art and design appear on a daily basis. We have listed some interesting sites below, but you should also do your own searching when you have free time. Searching for 'art magazine online', for example, will give you over a million starting points.

Aesthetica art magazine – www.aestheticamagazine.com
A List Apart (web design) – www.alistapart.com
Art UK – www.artuk.org
Artnet – www.artnet.com
Frieze – www.frieze.com
Google Arts and Culture – www.artsandculture.google.com
Hyperallergic – www.hyperallergic.com
Juxtapoz Art & Culture Magazine – www.juxtapoz.com
The Museum of Modern Art – www.moma.org
NY Arts – www.nyartsmagazine.net
Printmakers' resources and links – www.printmaker.co.uk/links.html
Tate Collection – www.tate.org.uk/art
Whitehot – www.whitehotmagazine.com

## Artists' websites

Geraint Evans: www.geraintevans.net
Fergus Hare: www.fergushare.net
Greg Ioannou: www.gregoristomazou.com; @ioannougreg
Anna Lytridou: www.annalytridou.com
Michael Milloy: @michael.milloy
Lucy Mullican: www.lucymullican.com
Johanna Parv: www.johannaparv.com

# Appendix 1: Institution contact details

**Aberystwyth University**
Tel: 01970 622021
Email: ug-admissions@aber.ac.uk
www.aber.ac.uk

**Accrington & Rossendale College**
Tel: 01254 389933
Email: admissions@nelsongroup.ac.uk
www.accross.ac.uk

**Activate Learning (Oxford, Reading, Banbury & Bicester)**
Tel: 0800 612 6008
Email: HE@activatelearning.ac.uk
www.activatelearning.ac.uk

**Anglia Ruskin University**
Tel: 01245 686868
Email: answers@aru.ac.uk
www.aru.ac.uk

**University of the Arts London**
Email: ucas.enquiries@arts.ac.uk
www.arts.ac.uk

**Arts University Bournemouth**
Tel: 01202 363228
Email: admissions@aub.ac.uk
www.aub.ac.uk

**Bangor University**
Tel: 01248 383717
Email: admissions@bangor.ac.uk
www.bangor.ac.uk

**Barking and Dagenham College**
Tel: 020 3667 0265
Email: admissions@bdc.ac.uk
www.barkingdagenhamcollege.ac.uk

**Barnet and Southgate College**
Tel: 020 8266 4000
Email: info@barnetsouthgate.ac.uk
www.barnetsouthgate.ac.uk

**Barnfield College, Luton**
Tel: 01582 569819
Email: admissions@barnfield.ac.uk
www.barnfield.ac.uk

**Barnsley College**
Tel: 01226 216216
Email: omlreception@barnsley.ac.uk
www.barnsley.ac.uk

**Basingstoke College of Technology**
Tel: 01256 306679
Email: nextyear@bcot.ac.uk
www.bcot.ac.uk

**University of Bath**
Tel: 01225 383019
Email: admissions@bath.ac.uk
www.bath.ac.uk/admissions

**Bath College**
Tel: 01225 312191
Email: info@bathcollege.ac.uk
www.bathcollege.ac.uk

**Bath Spa University**
Tel: 01225 875875
Email: admissions@bathspa.ac.uk
www.bathspa.ac.uk

**Bedford College**
Tel: 0345 658 8990
www.bedfordcollegegroup.ac.uk

**University of Bedfordshire**
Tel: 01582 743500
Email: admission@beds.ac.uk
www.beds.ac.uk

**Bexley College**
Tel: 020 5954 4000
Email: studenthub@lsec.ac.uk
www.lsec.ac.uk

**Birmingham City University**
Tel: 0121 331 6295
www.bcu.ac.uk

**Birmingham Metropolitan College**
Tel: 0121 446 4545
Email: he@bmetc.ac.uk
www.bmetc.ac.uk

**Bishop Burton College**
Tel: 01964 553000
Email: outreach@bishopburton.ac.uk
www.bishopburton.ac.uk

**Blackburn College**
Tel: 01254 292929
Email: admissions@blackburn.ac.uk
www.blackburn.ac.uk

**Blackpool and The Fylde College**
Tel: 01253 504322
Email: admissions@blackpool.ac.uk
www.blackpool.ac.uk

**University of Bolton**
Tel: 01204 903903
Email: study@bolton.ac.uk
www.bolton.ac.uk

**Bournemouth and Poole College**
Tel: 01202 205180
Email: he@thecollege.co.uk
www.thecollege.co.uk

**Bournemouth University**
Tel: 01202 961916
Email: askbu@bournemouth.ac.uk
www.bournemouth.ac.uk

**Bradford College**
Tel: 01274 088088
Email: admissions@bradfordcollege.ac.uk
www.bradfordcollege.ac.uk

**Bridgend College**
Tel: 01656 302251
Email: hello@bridgend.ac.uk
www.bridgend.ac.uk

**University of Brighton**
Tel: 01273 644644
Email: admissions@brighton.ac.uk
www.brighton.ac.uk

**City of Bristol College**
Tel: 0117 312 5143
Email: caroline.coombs@cityofbristol.ac.uk
www.cityofbristol.ac.uk

**Brunel University London**
Tel: 01895 274000
www.brunel.ac.uk

**The University of Buckingham**
Tel: 01280 820227
Email: admissions@buckingham.ac.uk
www.buckingham.ac.uk

Appendix 1

**Buckinghamshire College Group**
Tel: 01494 585503
Email: admissions@buckscollegegroup.ac.uk
www.buckscollegegroup.ac.uk

**Buckinghamshire New University**
Tel: 01494 605060
Email: admissions@bucks.ac.uk
www.bucks.ac.uk

**Bury College**
Tel: 0161 280 8200
Email: admissions@burycollege.ac.uk
www.burycollege.ac.uk

**Calderdale College**
Tel: 01422 399316
Email: admissions@calderdale.ac.uk
www.calderdale.ac.uk

**University of Cambridge**
Email: admissions@cam.ac.uk
www.study.cam.ac.uk

**Cambridge School of Visual & Performing Arts**
Tel: 01223 341300
Email: admissions@csvpa.com
www.csvpa.com

**Canterbury Christ Church University**
Tel: 01227 926000
Email: courses@canterbury.ac.uk
www.canterbury.ac.uk

**Canterbury College**
Tel: 01227 811111
Email: iag@eastkent.ac.uk
www.ekcgroup.ac.uk/colleges/canterbury-college

**Cardiff University**
Tel: 029 2087 9999
www.cardiff.ac.uk

**Cardiff Metropolitan University**
Tel: 029 2041 6010
Email: askadmissions@cardiffmet.ac.uk
www.cardiffmet.ac.uk

**Carshalton College**
Tel: 020 8544 4444
Email: admissions.carshalton@stcg.ac.uk
www.carshalton.ac.uk

**Cheshire College South & West**
Tel: 01270 654654
Email: info@ccsw.ac.uk
www.ccsw.ac.uk

**University of Chester**
Tel: 01244 511000
Email: admissions@chester.ac.uk
www.chester.ac.uk

**Chesterfield College**
Tel: 01246 500500
Email: admissions@chesterfield.ac.uk
www.chesterfield.ac.uk

**University of Chichester**
Tel: 01243 816000
Email: admissions@chi.ac.uk
www.chi.ac.uk

**Chichester College**
Tel: 01243 786321
Email: info@chichester.ac.uk
www.chichester.ac.uk

**City and Islington College (London)**
Tel: 020 7963 4181
Email: candiapplicationsupport@candi.ac.uk
www.candi.ac.uk/higher-education

**City College Plymouth**
Tel: 01752 305300
Email: info@cityplym.ac.uk
www.cityplym.ac.uk

**City of Glasgow College**
Tel: 0141 375 5555
Email: enquiries@cityofglasgow.ac.uk
www.cityofglasgowcollege.ac.uk

**The City of Liverpool College**
Tel: 0151 2521515
Email: enquiry@liv-coll.ac.uk
www.liv-coll.ac.uk

**City of Westminster College**
Tel: 020 7723 8826
Email: customer.services@cwc.ac.uk
www.cwc.ac.uk

**City of Wolverhampton College**
Tel: 01902 836000
www.wolvcoll.ac.uk

**Colchester Institute**
Tel: 01206 712777
www.colchester.ac.uk

**Cornwall College**
Tel: 01209 617698
www.cornwall.ac.uk

**Coventry University**
Tel: 024 7765 2222
Email: ukadmissions@coventry.ac.uk
www.coventry.ac.uk

**Craven College**
Tel: 01756 791411
Email: enquiries@craven-college.ac.uk
www.craven-college.ac.uk

**University for the Creative Arts (UCA)**
Tel: 01252 918291
Email: enquiries@uca.ac.uk
www.uca@ac.uk

**Croydon College**
Tel: 020 8686 5700
Email: admissions@croydon.ac.uk
www.croydon.ac.uk

**University of Cumbria**
Tel: 0808 178 7373
Email: enquirycentre@cumbria.ac.uk
www.cumbria.ac.uk

**De Montfort University (Leicester)**
Tel: 0116 250 6070
Email: enquiry@dmu.ac.uk
www.dmu.ac.uk

**University of Derby**
Tel: 01332 591167
Email: askadmissions@derby.ac.uk
www.derby.ac.uk

**Doncaster College**
Tel: 0800 358 7575
Email: dcinfocentre@don.ac.uk
www.don.ac.uk

**Dudley College of Technology**
Tel: 01384 363333
Email: admissions@dudleycol.ac.uk
www.dudleycol.ac.uk

**University of Dundee**
Tel: 01382 383838
www.dundee.ac.uk/study/ug

**University of East Anglia (UEA)**
Tel: 01603 591515
Email: admissions@uea.ac.uk
www.uea.ac.uk

**University of East London (UEL)**
Tel: 020 8223 3333
Email: study@uel.ac.uk
www.uel.ac.uk

**East Riding College**
Tel: 0345 120 0044
Email: admissions@eastridingcollege.ac.uk
www.eastridingcollege.ac.uk

Appendix 1

**East Surrey College**
Tel: 01737 772611
Email: clientservices@esc.ac.uk
www.esc.ac.uk

**East Sussex College**
Tel: 030 3003 9699
www.escg.ac.uk

**The University of Edinburgh**
Tel: 0131 650 4360
Email: sra.enquiries@ed.ac.uk
www.ed.ac.uk

**Edinburgh Napier University**
Tel: 0333 900 6040
Email: studentrecruitment@napier.ac.uk
www.napier.ac.uk

**Exeter College**
Tel: 01392 400500
Email: info@exe-coll.ac.uk
www.exe-coll.ac.uk/he

**Falmouth University**
Tel: 01326 213730
Email: applicantservices@falmouth.ac.uk
www.falmouth.ac.uk/admissions

**University Centre Farnborough**
Tel: 01252 407028
Email: admissions@farn-ct.ac.uk
www.farn-ct.ac.uk

**Furness College**
Tel: 01229 8250117
Email: info@furness.ac.uk
www.furness.ac.uk

**Gateshead College**
Tel: 0191 490 2246
Email: start@gateshead.ac.uk
www.gateshead.ac.uk

**Glasgow Caledonian University**
Tel: 0141 331 8630
Email: ukroenquiries@gcu.ac.uk
www.gcu.ac.uk

**The Glasgow School of Art**
Tel: 0141 353 4500
Email: admissions@gsa.ac.uk
www.gsa.ac.uk

**The University of Gloucestershire**
Tel: 0333 014 1141
Email: admissions@glos.ac.uk
www.glos.ac.uk

**Gloucestershire College**
Tel: 0345 155 2020
Email: info@gloscol.ac.uk
www.gloscol.ac.uk

**Goldsmiths, University of London**
Tel: 020 7919 7171
Email: admissions@gold.ac.uk
www.gold.ac.uk

**Gower College Swansea**
Tel: 01792 284179
Email: fiona.john@gowercollegeswansea.ac.uk
www.gowercollegeswansea.ac.uk

**Greater Brighton Metropolitan College**
Tel: 01273 667704
Email: admissions@gbmc.ac.uk
www.gbmc.ac.uk

**University of Greenwich**
Tel: 020 8331 9000
Email: courseinfo@gre.ac.uk
www.gre.ac.uk

**University Centre Grimsby**
Tel: 0800 328 3631
Email: headmissions@grimsby.ac.uk
www.grimsby.ac.uk

**Guildford College**
Tel: 0800 612 6008
www.guildford.activelearning.ac.uk

**Harrogate College**
Tel: 01423 879466
Email: contact@harrogate-college.ac.uk
www.harrogate-college.ac.uk

**Heart of Worcestershire College**
Tel: 01905 743456
Email: admissions-worcester@howcollege.ac.uk
www.howcollege.ac.uk

**Hereford College of Arts**
Tel: 01432 273359
Email: enquiries@hca.ac.uk
www.hca.ac.uk

**Heriot-Watt University, Edinburgh**
Tel: 01856 850605
Email: icit@hw.ac.uk
www.hw.ac.uk

**University of Hertfordshire**
Tel: 01707 284800
Email: ask@herts.ac.uk
www.herts.ac.uk

**University of the Highlands and Islands**
Tel: 01463 279190
Email: info@uhi.ac.uk
www.uhi.ac.uk

**The University of Huddersfield**
Tel: 01484 473969
Email: admissionsandrecords@hud.ac.uk
www.hud.ac.uk

**Hugh Baird College**
Tel: 0151 353 4444
Email: enquiries@hughbaird.ac.uk
www.hughbaird.ac.uk/index.php/university-centre

**The University of Hull**
Tel: 01482 466100
Email: admissions@hull.ac.uk
www.hull.ac.uk

**Hull College**
Tel: 01482 329943
Email: info@hull-college.ac.uk
www.hull-college.ac.uk/HE

**The University of Kent**
Tel: 01227 764000
www.kent.ac.uk

**Kingston College**
Tel: 020 8546 2152
Email: info.kingston@stcg.ac.uk.
www.stcg.ac.uk

**Kingston University**
Tel: 020 3308 9932
Email: admissionssops@kingston.ac.uk
www.kingston.ac.uk

**Kirklees College**
Tel: 01484 437000
Email: info@kirkleescollege.ac.uk
www.kirkleescollege.ac.uk

**KLC School of Design (London)**
Tel: 020 7376 3377
Email: info@klc.co.uk
www.klc.co.uk

**Lakes College – West Cumbria**
Tel: 01946 839300
Email: info@lcwc.ac.uk
www.lcwc.ac.uk

**University of Central Lancashire (UCLan)**
Tel: 01772 892444
Email: admissions@uclan.ac.uk
www.uclan.ac.uk

**Lancaster University**
Tel: 01524 65201
Email: ugadmissions@lancaster.ac.uk
www.lancaster.ac.uk

**University of Leeds**
Tel: 0113 243 1751
Email: study@leeds.ac.uk
www.leeds.ac.uk

**Leeds Beckett University**
Tel: 0113 812 3113
Email: admissionenquiries@leedsbeckett.ac.uk
www.leedsbeckett.ac.uk

**Leeds City College**
Tel: 0113 386 1997
Email: contact@leedscitycollege.ac.uk
www.leedscitycollege.ac.uk

**Leeds College of Art**
Tel.: 0113 202 8000
Email: admissions@leeds-art.ac.uk
www.leeds-art.ac.uk

**Leeds College of Building**
Tel: 0113 222 6002
Email: info@lcb.ac.uk
www.lcb.ac.uk

**University of Leicester**
Tel: 0116 252 2522
Email: admissions@le.ac.uk
www.le.ac.uk

**Leicester College**
Tel: 0116 224 2240
www.leicestercollege.ac.uk

**Lewisham Southwark College**
Tel: 020 3757 3000
Email: info@lewisham.ac.uk
www.lewisham.ac.uk

**University of Lincoln**
Tel: 01522 882000
Email: enquiries@lincoln.ac.uk
www.lincoln.ac.uk

**Lincoln College**
Tel: 030 0303 2435
Email: enquiries@lincolncollege.ac.uk
www.lincolncollege.ac.uk

**University of Liverpool**
Tel: 0151 794 5927
Email: irro@liverpool.ac.uk
www.liv.ac.uk

**Liverpool Hope University**
Tel: 0151 291 3111
Email: enquiry@hope.ac.uk
www.hope.ac.uk

**The Liverpool Institute for Performing Arts**
Tel: 0151 330 3084
Email: admissions@lipa.ac.uk
www.lipa.ac.uk

**Liverpool John Moores University (LJMU)**
Tel: 0151 231 5090
Email: courses@ljmu.ac.uk
www.ljmu.ac.uk

**Coleg Llandrillo**
Tel: 01492 542338
Email: generalenquiries@gllm.ac.uk
www.gllm.ac.uk

**ARU London (LCA Business School)**
Tel: 020 7400 6789
Email: enquiry@london.aru.ac.uk
https://lca.anglia.ac.uk

**The London College, UCK**
Tel: 020 7243 4000
Email: admissions@lcuck.ac.uk
www.lcuck.ac.uk

**London Metropolitan University**
Tel: 020 7133 4200
www.londonmet.ac.uk

**London South Bank University**
Tel: 020 7815 7500
www.lsbu.ac.uk

**Loughborough University**
Tel: 01509 222222
Email: enquiriess@lboro.ac.uk
www.lboro.ac.uk

**The University of Manchester**
Tel: 0161 275 2077
Email: study@manchester.ac.uk
www.manchester.ac.uk

**The Manchester College**
Tel: 0333 322 2444
Email: enquiries@tmc.ac.uk
www.tmc.ac.uk

**Manchester Metropolitan University**
Tel: 0161 247 2000
www.mmu.ac.uk

**Coleg Menai**
Tel: 01492 542338
Email: generalenquiries@gllm.ac.uk
www.gllm.ac.uk

**Middlesex University**
Tel: 020 8411 5555
www.mdx.ac.uk

**Milton Keynes College**
Tel: 01908 684444
Email:admissionsandenrolments@mkcollege.ac.uk
www.mkcollege.ac.uk

**Mont Rose College**
Tel: 020 8556 5009
Email: info@mrcollege.ac.uk
www.mrcollege.ac.uk

**Morley College London**
Tel: 020 7450 1889
www.morleycollege.ac.uk

**Newcastle College**
Tel: 0191 200 4000
Email: enquiries@ncl-coll.ac.uk
www.newcastlecollege.co.uk

**Newcastle University**
Tel: 0191 208 6000
www.ncl.ac.uk

**New City College**
Tel: 0330 135 9000
Email:info@nncclondon.ac.uk
www.ncclondon.ac.uk

**New College Durham**
Tel: 0191 375 4210
Email: admissions@newdur.ac.uk
www.newcollegedurham.ac.uk

**New College of the Humanities**
Tel: 020 7637 4550
Email: info@nulondon.ac.uk
www.nulondon.ac.uk

**New College Swindon**
Tel: 01793 611470
Email: info@newcollege.ac.uk
www.newcollege.ac.uk

**North Lindsey College**
Tel: 01724 294125
Email: enquiries@ucnl.ac.uk
www.northlindsey.ac.uk

**North Warwickshire & South Leicestershire College**
Tel: 0330 058 3000
Email: enquiries@nwslc.ac.uk
www.nwslc.ac.uk

**University of Northampton**
Tel: 0300 303 2772
Email: admissions@northampton.ac.uk
www.northampton.ac.uk

**Northern School of Art**
Tel: 01642 288888
Email: studentrecruitment@northernart.ac.uk
www.northernart.ac.uk

**Northumberland College**
Tel: 0330 770 6000
Email: info@northland.ac.uk
www.northumberland.ac.uk

**Northumbria University**
Tel: 0191 406 0901
Email: bc.applicantservices@northumbria.ac.uk
www.northumbria.ac.uk

Appendix 1

**Norwich University of The Arts**
Tel: 01603 610561
Email: studentrecruitment@nua.ac.uk
www.nua.ac.uk

**Nottingham College**
Tel: 0115 9100 100
Email: enquiries@nottinghamcollege.ac.uk
www.nottinghamcollege.ac.uk

**The University of Nottingham**
Tel: 0115 951 5151
www.nottingham.ac.uk

**Nottingham Trent University**
Tel: 0115 848 4200
Email: enquiries@ntu.ac.uk
www.ntu.ac.uk

**Oaklands College**
Tel: 01727 737000
Email: info@oaklands.ac.uk
www.oaklands.ac.uk

**University Campus Oldham**
Tel: 0161 344 8800
Email: info@uco.oldham.ac.uk
www.uco.oldham.ac.uk

**Oxford Brookes University**
Tel: 0345 350 3699
Email: admissions@brookes.ac.uk
www.brookes.ac.uk

**Oxford University**
Tel: 01865 270000
www.ox.ac.uk/apply

**Pearson College London**
Tel: 020 3930 4802
Email: info@pearsoncollegelondon.ac.uk
www.pearsoncollege.com

**Petroc**
Tel: 01271 345291
Email: reception@petroc.ac.uk
www.petroc.ac.uk

**Plumpton College**
Tel: 01273 890454
www.plumpton.ac.uk

**Plymouth College of Art**
Tel: 01752 203400
Email: admissions@pca.ac.uk
www.plymouthart.ac.uk

**University of Plymouth**
Tel: 01752 585858
Email: admissions@plymouth.ac.uk
www.plymouth.ac.uk

**University of Portsmouth**
Tel: 023 9284 5566
Email: admissions@port.ac.uk
www.port.ac.uk

**Queen's University Belfast**
Tel: 028 9097 3838
Email: admissions@qub.ac.uk
www.qub.ac.uk

**Queen Mary University of London**
Tel: 020 7882 5511
Email: admissions@qmul.ac.uk
www.qmul.ac.uk

**Ravensbourne**
Tel: 020 3040 3500
Email: hello@rave.ac.uk
www.ravensbourne.ac.uk

**University of Reading**
Tel: 0118 378 8372
Email: ugadmissions@reading.ac.uk
www.reading.ac.uk

**Regent's University London**
Tel: 020 7487 7625
Email: admit@regents.ac.uk
www.regents.ac.uk

**Robert Gordon University**
Tel: 01224 262000
Email: admissions@rgu.ac.uk
www.rgu.ac.uk

**University of Roehampton**
Tel: 020 8392 3232
Email: enquiries@roehampton.ac.uk
www.roehampton.ac.uk

**Rose Bruford College**
Tel: 020 8308 2600
Email: enquiries@bruford.ac.uk
www.bruford.ac.uk

**Rotherham College**
Tel: 01709 362111
Email: info@rotherham.ac.uk
www.rotherham.ac.uk

**Royal Central School of Speech and Drama, University of London**
Tel: 020 7722 8183
Email: admissions@cssd.ac.uk
www.cssd.ac.uk

**Royal Conservatoire of Scotland**
Tel: 0141 332 4101
Email: admissions@rcs.ac.uk
www.rcs.ac.uk

**Runshaw College**
Tel: 01772 642040
Email: justaskr@runshaw.ac.uk
www.runshaw.ac.uk

**Ruskin College Oxford**
Tel: 01865 759600
Email: enquiries@ruskin.ac.uk
www.ruskin.ac.uk

**SAE Institute**
Tel: 0333 011 2315
Email: ukadmissions@sae.edu
www.sae.edu

**The University of Salford**
Tel: 0161 295 5000
Email: course-enquiries@salford.ac.uk
www.salford.ac.uk

**Selby College**
Tel: 01757 211000
Email: info@selby.ac.uk
www.selby.ac.uk

**The University of Sheffield**
Tel: 0114 222 2000
Email: shefapply@sheffield.ac.uk
www.sheffield.ac.uk

**Sheffield College**
Tel: 0114 260 2600
Email: info@sheffcol.ac.uk
www.sheffcol.ac.uk

**Sheffield Hallam University**
Tel: 0114 225 5555
Email: enquiries@shu.ac.uk
www.shu.ac.uk

**Shrewsbury Colleges Group**
Email: info@scg.ac.uk
www.scg.ac.uk

**Coleg Sir Gâr/Carmarthenshire College**
Tel: 01554 748000
Email: admissions@colegsirgar.ac.uk
www.colegsirgar.ac.uk

**Solihull College**
Tel: 0121 678 7000
Email: enquiries@solihull.ac.uk
www.solihull.ac.uk

**Somerset College**
Tel: 01278 455464
Email: info@somerset.ac.uk
www.somerset.ac.uk

**South and City College Birmingham**
Tel: 0121 694 5000
Email: admissions@sccb.ac.uk
www.sccb.ac.uk

**University of Southampton**
Tel: 023 8059 5000
Email: enquiries@southampton.ac.uk
www.southampton.ac.uk

# Appendix 1

**Southampton Solent University**
Tel: 023 8201 5066
Email: admissions@solent.ac.uk
www.solent.ac.uk

**South Devon College**
Tel: 0800 0380 123
Email: enquiries@southdevon.ac.uk
www.southdevon.ac.uk

**South Essex College**
Tel: 0345 521 2345
Email: learning@southessex.ac.uk
www.southessex.ac.uk

**South Gloucestershire and Stroud College**
Tel: 0800 0567 253
Email: info@sgscol.ac.uk
www.sgscol.ac.uk

**South Thames College**
Tel: 020 8918 7777
Email: info@south-thames.ac.uk
www.south-thames.ac.uk

**South Tyneside College**
Tel: 0191 427 3500
Email: student.services@stc.ac.uk
www.stc.ac.uk

**Southport College**
Tel: 01704 392704
Email: guidance@southport.ac.uk
www.southport.ac.uk

**University of South Wales**
Tel: 03455 767778
www.southwales.ac.uk

**Spurgeon's College**
Tel: 020 8683 8462
Email: enquiries@spurgeons.ac.uk
www.spurgeons.ac.uk

**Staffordshire University**
Tel: 01782 294000
www.staffs.ac.uk

**Stamford College**
Tel: 01780 484300
Email: enquiries@stamford.ac.uk
www.stamford.ac.uk

**Stockport College**
Tel: 0161 296 5000
Email: heenquiries@tcg.ac.uk
www.stockport.ac.uk

**University Centre St Helens**
Tel: 01744 733766
Email: enquire@sthelens.ac.uk
www.sthelens.ac.uk

**The University of Strathclyde**
Tel: 0141 552 4400
Email: ug.admissions@strath.ac.uk
www.strath.ac.uk

**University Campus Suffolk (UCS)**
Tel: 01473 338833
www.ucs.ac.uk

**Sunderland College**
Tel: 0300 770 8000
Email: info@sunderlandcollege.ac.uk
www.sunderlandcollege.ac.uk

**University of Sunderland**
Tel: 0191 515 2000
Email: student.helpline@sunderland.ac.uk
www.sunderland.ac.uk

**University of Surrey**
Tel: 01483 682222
www.surrey.ac.uk

**Teesside University**
Tel: 01642 218121
Email: enquiries@tees.ac.uk
www.tees.ac.uk

**Truro and Penwith College**
Tel: 01872 305000
Email: enquiry@truro-penwith.ac.uk
www.truro-penwith.ac.uk

**Tyne Metropolitan College**
Tel: 0191 229 5000
Email: enquiries@tynemet.ac.uk
www.tynemet.ac.uk

**UCL (University College London)**
Tel: 020 7679 3000
www.ucl.ac.uk

**Ulster University**
Tel: 028 9536 5117
Email: r.cullen@ulster.ac.uk
www.ulster.ac.uk

**Wakefield College**
Tel: 01924 789789
Email: info@wakefield.ac.uk
www.wakefield.ac.uk

**University of Wales Trinity St David**
Tel: 0300 500 5054
Email: admissions@uwtsd.ac.uk
www.uwtsd.ac.uk

**University of Wales Trinity St David (UWTSD Swansea)**
Tel: 01792 481000
Email: admissions@uwtsd.ac.uk
www.uwtsd.ac.uk

**Walsall College**
Tel: 01922 657000
www.walsallcollege.ac.uk

**Warrington Collegiate**
Tel: 01925 494400
Email: learner.services@warrington.ac.uk
www.warrington.ac.uk

**Warrington and Vale Royal College**
Tel: 01925 494494
Email: learner.services@wvr.ac.uk
www.wvr.ac.uk

**Warwickshire College Group**
Tel: 0300 456 0049
Email: info@warwickshire.ac.uk
www.wcg.ac.uk

**West London College**
Tel: 020 8741 1688
Email: lis@wlc.ac.uk
www.wlc.ac.uk

**University of West London**
Tel: 0800 036 8888
Email: courses@uwl.ac.uk
www.uwl.ac.uk

**University of the West of England, Bristol (UWE)**
Tel: 0117 328 3333
Email: admissions@uwe.ac.uk
www.uwe.ac.uk

**University of the West of Scotland**
Tel: 0800 027 1000
Email: ask@uws.ac.uk
www.uws.ac.uk

**University of Westminster**
Tel: 020 7915 5000
Email: course-enquiries@westminster.ac.uk
www.westminster.ac.uk

**Weston College**
Tel: 01934 411411
www.weston.ac.uk

**Weymouth College**
Tel: 01305 761100
Email: sue-dafter@weymouth.ac.uk
www.weymouth.ac.uk

**Wigan and Leigh College**
Tel: 01942 761600
Email: applications@wigan-leigh.ac.uk
www.wigan-leigh.ac.uk

**Wirral Metropolitan College**
Tel: 0151 551 7777
Email: wmc.enquiries@wmc.ac.uk
www.wmc.ac.uk

**University of Wolverhampton**
Tel: 01902 323505
Email: admissions@wlv.ac.uk
www.wlv.ac.uk

**University of Worcester**
Tel: 01905 855111
Email: admissions@worc.ac.uk
www.worcester.ac.uk

**Wrexham University**
Tel: 01978 293439
Email: enquiries@wrexham.ac.uk
www.wrexham.ac.uk

**Writtle College**
Tel: 01245 424200
Email: admissions@writtle.ac.uk
www.writtle.ac.uk

**Yeovil College**
Tel: 01935 845454
Email: university.centre@yeovil.ac.uk
www.yeovil.ac.uk

**University of York**
Tel: 01904 324000
Email: ug-admissions@york.ac.uk
www.york.ac.uk

**York College**
Tel: 01904 770100
Email: info@yorkcollege.ac.uk
www.yorkcollege.ac.uk

**York St John University**
Tel: 01904 876598
Email: admissions@yorksj.ac.uk
www.yorksj.ac.uk

The colleges and universities in Appendix 1 are listed on the UCAS website as they offer Higher Education courses (HND courses, degree and Foundation degree courses). Some Foundation providers offer Further Education courses only and so are not listed. Direct applications for these colleges can be made through their websites. The University of the Arts London comprises six colleges: Central Saint Martins, Chelsea School of Art, London College of Communication, Wimbledon School of Art, Camberwell School of Art and London College of Fashion; courses offered by these colleges are listed under the University of the Arts course details.

# Appendix 2: Glossary

## Studying art and design

**Art Foundation**
A one-year further education course offered by universities and colleges, commonly taken by students who want to apply for art or design degree courses at university.

**Art school**
University departments of art and/or design and stand-alone colleges specialising in the teaching of art and design are commonly referred to as art schools.

**Clearing**
Students who have applied for degree courses but either have no offers or who have not achieved the required grades for their offers in August can use the UCAS Clearing scheme to apply to other universities.

**Extra**
Students who have applied for degree courses but who receive no offers can approach more universities from February of the year they intend to go to university using the UCAS Extra system.

**Foundation degree**
A two-year higher education course.

**Further education course**
A course below degree level, such as a Foundation course.

**Higher education course**
A degree-level course.

**Higher National Diploma (HND)**
A higher education course, often of two years' duration. On some HND courses, students can add a third year to reach degree level.

**Portfolio**
This can refer either to the case in which an artist carries his or her work or to a body of work that represents the artist's areas of specialisation or interest.

Appendix 2

**UCAS**
The Universities and Colleges Admissions Service, the centralised university applications system for degree course applications.

**UCAS Postgraduate**
The UCAS system for postgraduate applications to selected universities.

# Ways of describing art and design

*(NB: these are general descriptions, not definitions, and there are as many ways of categorising types of art and design as there are styles of art itself – and no two people will ever agree on exact definitions.)*

**Abstract art**
Art that relies on colour, shape and form to evoke feelings and emotions; or to express ideas.

**Architecture**
The design of structures and buildings.

**Art**
What is art? A good question, and one that people have been asking ever since prehistoric man drew pictures of animals on cave walls. For many people, art is a way of communicating their hopes, fears, beliefs or feelings in a predominantly visual way.

**Art history**
The study of how changes in styles of painting, sculpture and architecture throughout history relate to or are caused by social, technological or political changes and events.

**Ceramics**
The design and creation of objects using clay or related materials.

**Conceptual art**
A work of art in which the idea behind the piece is more important than the actual piece itself.

**Contextual studies**
The study of the theory of art, taking into account political and social influences, the use of materials and techniques.

**Crafts**
Work created in studios that has a practical use, such as pottery, jewellery and glassware, typically handmade.

### Design
Designers create things or ideas that can be used for practical purposes, for example websites, furniture and clothing.

### Environmental art
Art created out of natural materials as part of the landscape.

### Fashion
The design and production of clothes, shoes or accessories, such as handbags.

### Figurative art
Art that recognisably depicts people or things.

### Fine art
Fine art courses cover the traditional elements of art, such as painting, drawing and sculpture. Fine art practitioners generally focus on producing works that create emotional responses rather than having practical uses.

### Performance art
Art that relies on the artist using him- or herself, or other participants, as the artwork.

### Photography
The use of light to create still or moving images on light-sensitive surfaces. Photography courses can include film and video.

### Printmaking
Creating images by transferring ink or other pigments onto paper, cloth or other surfaces using another surface, such as wood, etched metals, silk screens, etc.

### Textiles
Creating cloth using techniques such as felt-making, knitting and weaving.

# Have you seen the rest of the Getting into series?

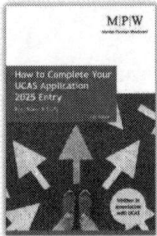

Written by experts in a clear and concise format, these guides go beyond the official publications to give you practical advice on how to secure a place on the course of your choice.

Order today from
www.trotman.co.uk/GettingInto